"Ignorance of the law excuses no man; not that all me   , ~~but~~ because it is an excuse every man will plead, and no man can tell how to confute him." **John Selden**

"Who will protect the public when the police violate the law?" **William Ramsey Clark**

Though every one of us is affected in some way by the justice system, very few of us actually understand the justice system and criminal laws. That's fine until we find ourselves or our loved ones caught in the system. Once you're caught in the justice system, the chances of things turning out for the best are severely diminished. The best way to beat the system is to avoid getting caught up in the system in the first place. That's where *When The Cops Come Knockin'* comes in.

The basic premise of this book is that an ounce of prevention is worth a pound of the cure. Like getting vaccinated against catching a horrible disease in the future, knowing the law and protecting your rights can prevent horrible legal consequences in the future. Those consequences can range from financial troubles like those associated with posting expensive bond and paying astronomically high lawyer fees, to mental and emotional stresses like those that come with being arrested and going to trial. Of course, the worst consequences are ultimately imprisonment or even death. The nominal cost of this book pales in comparison to those costs. Arming yourself with the information inside this book is no different than getting a booster shot. Except that instead of disease prevention, this book's aim is to protect you from the illnesses of the criminal justice system.

Now you don't have to spend hours on end at your local law library, attend law school, or hire an attorney to explain criminal law to you. Much of the same information that it would take days or even weeks for a non lawyer to find is available for you in this easy-to-understand book.

When The Cops Come Knockin' is a worst-case interpretation of complex criminal law and procedure concepts. These concepts are put into plain English for all to understand. The content of this book includes simple explanations of your rights, and descriptions of laws under which many people serve prison time. *When The Cops Come Knockin'* also discusses defenses to criminal charges, provides guidance on how to behave when coming into contact with the police, and suggests strategies for living a law-abiding life. Through words and illustrations, we use real-world examples to help readers understand difficult concepts of criminal law and procedure. We also show readers how criminal law plays out in situations that they experience everyday, sometimes without even knowing it.

In line with our goal of making things easy for the reader, here we outline exactly what you will see in *When The Cops Come Knockin'*. First, as a general matter, we use slang and some real talk to make it simple and easy for you to understand. Second, you will find illustrations to help you better understand the concepts we explain or points we make. By choosing these methods to get the concepts across, we are in no way attempting to degrade, offend or disrespect anybody or any group of people, nor are we attempting to promote the use of such devices. We believe that this is simply one effective way to communicate our message to the broadest cross-section of people. Third, we will discuss what it takes to commit and be charged with a crime. Fourth, we will discuss defenses to criminal charges. Fifth, we will explain to you the rights you *do not* have, meaning things that law enforcement representatives can do to you without you having any way to stop them. Lastly, we will talk about the rights you *do* have and how you can assert them so your rights are not violated by law enforcement.

WHEN THE COPS COME KNOCKIN'

An Illustrated Guide to Criminal Law

by

Travis Townsend and Trinity Townsend

Torinity, LLC.
College Park, GA

First Printing 2008
10 9 8 7 6 5 4 3 2 1

ISBN: 9780615278858

Library of Congress Control Number: 2008910223

Torinity, LLC.
College Park, GA
1-800-552-0762, ext 500

Disclaimer:

WARNING! THE EXPLANATIONS PROVIDED THROUGHOUT WHEN THE COPS COME KNOCKIN' ARE NOT INTENDED TO BE PRECISE RECITATIONS OF THE LAW, BUT INSTEAD ARE LOOSE, WORST-CASE SCENARIO TRANSLATIONS OF THE LAW AIMED AT GIVING THE READER A SURFACE UNDERSTANDING OF THE LAW. THE DEFINITIONS OF SPECIFIED LAWS IN THIS BOOK ARE LOOSELY BASED ON THE MODEL PENAL CODE AND COMMON LAW, AND MAY NOT BE IN EFFECT IN THE JURISDICTION AND CITY APPLICABLE TO YOU. BY WRITING THIS BOOK, WE ARE NOT PROVIDING LEGAL ADVICE AND DO NOT ATTEMPT TO PROVIDE LEGAL ADVICE. READERS ASSUME THE RISK OF ACTING UPON THE INFORMATION FOUND IN WHEN THE COPS COME KNOCKIN'. WE RECOMMEND YOU CONTACT AN ATTORNEY WITH RESPECT TO ANY AND ALL THE SUBJECT MATTER INSIDE THIS BOOK FOR CLARIFICATION, AND IF YOU FIND YOURSELF IN LEGAL TROUBLE, HIRE AN ATTORNEY IMMEDIATELY OR IF YOU CAN'T AFFORD ONE, ASK TO HAVE THE COURT APPOINT AN ATTORNEY TO YOU IMMEDIATELY!

ACKNOWLEDGEMENTS

Numerous people were helpful and supportive in the production and development of this book.

Our thanks:

To Joann Odneal, Travis Townsend, Sr., Keith Townsend, Stephanie Massey, all our extended Townsend and Curry family, Charlene Brown, Delvon Parker, Stephanie Meister, Jon Royce, Sheri-McCurdy-Knox, Eric Simon, Lashay Callaway, Willie Raby, Michael Griffin, Paul Castenada, Justice Barber, Brandon Williams, Cassandra Tucker, Robert Reid, Andre Hewitt, Martha Duncan, Dwyone Joiner, Tamera Woodard, Shauna Hill, Julia Trankiem, Selia Acevedo, Deidre Frances, Yale Kamisar, Robert Daniel, Brooke Reynolds, Christopher Reynolds, Kenneth Turk, Felicia LeRay, Diego Bernal, James Forman, Jr. and Bernard Coleman.

To illustrator and cover designer Sean Forney.

To layout and design specialist Bob Spear.

To designer Colin Quashie.

Any and all errors and omissions are, of course, entirely attributable to the authors.

TABLE OF CONTENTS

DEFINITIONS

Civil penalty	A fine or fee that you have to pay to the government for committing violations of the law.
Commission of a crime	Doing things that are against the law. For example, stealing is against the law. Grabbing a candy bar from a gas station and leaving without paying for it is the commission of a crime.
Convicted/Conviction	When the judge or jury decide that somebody has actually committed a crime, that person is convicted of that crime and will be sentenced as punishment for that crime.
Cop (not police)	Normally, the word cop is used to define a police officer. We sometimes use the word cop in "When The Cops Come Knockin'" to mean "to go and buy something." For example, if you cop some new sneakers, that means you purchased some new sneakers.
Court	The place where hearings, trials and other criminal proceedings are held. The term court is also used to refer to the judge, especially when we say, "the court says."
Defense	The story or angle a person on trial for a crime uses to keep from being charged with some or all of the charges against him.
Drug paraphernalia	Anything related to drug use and drug dealing. This includes drugs, needles, bags for packaging, pots used to cook drugs, scales, pipes and bongs, papers for rolling, pill bottles, and everything else connected to the drug world.
Drug trafficking	Selling or transporting illegal drugs in large amounts, or over long distances.
Element of a crime	Any part of what it takes to commit a crime. For example, the elements of 1st degree murder are 1) intentionally, 2) doing an action, 3) that causes, 4) the unjustifiable death of 5) another person.
Fence	A person who sells stolen goods for a thief. The word fence is also defined as the act of taking stolen goods and selling them.

Frown upon	To look at badly, or look down on. For example, people frown upon cracking jokes on disabled people.
Infamous	Well-known for trouble or criminal activity. The guy in your hood that everybody is afraid of because he's known for beating people down is infamous.
Judge	The ruler of your case and trial. This person is usually dressed in a black robe and has complete control over his/her courtroom. This person makes decisions about things that can and can't happen to you, and about how things are going to go for or against you. You must respect this person at all times.
Jury	Regular everyday people picked to decide your case. This means they decide if you go to jail or not depending on whether they believe your story or the prosecutor's (see below for more on the prosecutor).
Loot	To steal. Loot is also used to describe the stuff that has been stolen. For example, people were looting after Hurricane Katrina. The stolen stuff was called loot.
Narc	A police officer or informant that works for the government's drug enforcement department.
Narcotics	Illegal drugs.
Omission	Something that is supposed to happen, but doesn't happen, or something that is supposed to be included, but isn't included. For example, if you are supposed to bring your white T-shirt to wear under your jersey at the football game, leaving the shirt at home is an omission because you were supposed to bring it and you didn't.
Parole	Early release from prison under conditions. When somebody is let out on parole, they are still serving their prison sentence, but are allowed to do the rest of their time out of prison and have to follow strict rules. If they break those rules, their parole officer (see below for more on the parole officer) can send them straight back to prison for the rest of their sentence without another trial.
Parole officer	An employee of the federal or state government responsible for watching over you if you are allowed out of jail early on parole.
Perpetrator/Perp	A person who commits a crime. The robber in a robbery is the perpetrator. The drug dealer dealing drugs is the perpetrator. The person setting the house on fire in an arson case is the perpetrator.

Probation	When you've been found guilty of a crime but the judge decides to let you spend some or all of your sentence out of lock-up under strict watch by a probation officer (see below for more on the probation officer) to make sure that you keep your nose clean and follow strict rules. If you break the rules of your probation, your probation officer can send you to prison without another trial.
Probation officer	An employee of the federal or state government responsible for watching over you if you are convicted of a crime, not sentenced to jail, but put on probation instead.
Prosecution/ Prosecutor	The lawyer who tries to put you in jail. This lawyer represents the federal, state or local government and works closely with the police.
Provoke	To do something to cause a reaction from somebody or something. If you jump up and slap somebody in the face, you are provoking him to kick your butt.
Provocation	The thing done that causes a reaction from somebody or something. If you jump up and slap him in the face provoking him to knock you out, slapping them in the face is the provocation for the beat down you receive.
Ridin' dirty	Driving with drugs, other illegal stuff or without one or all of the following: license/registration/insurance.
Run (not racing or jogging)	To rob somebody or get robbed. For example, a robber makes his victim run his stuff and the robber leaves with it. Also, the victim runs his stuff for the robber and the robber leaves with it. The word "run" used in the robbery example applies to action taken by the robber and the victim.
Sobriety	The level of drunkenness or non-drunkenness you experience after drinking.
Voluntary	Without anybody forcing you. Children do work around the house because their parents make them so its not voluntary. When you wake up and cut the Play Station on without being told to do so, that's voluntary.
Willful blindness	Purposely not finding out all the facts about something so you can say you didn't know what was going on.

Cast of Characters

The People

Malcolm

Zeb

Carlos

Rob

Tamika

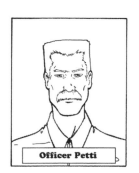
Bunny

The Law

Officer Grimes

Officer Petti

INTRODUCTION

Just about everybody is familiar with crime. You can't turn on the TV without hearing about it. The funny thing is, most people don't really understand criminal law. Wondering why YOU should care about criminal law? We could answer that question by going on and on about how the system victimizes ignorant people, but that would bore the hell out of you. Just know that understanding criminal law can save you hundreds to thousands of dollars in legal fees. It can save your family the heartbreak of watching you get caught up in the "system". Last, and most important, it can save YOU from going to jail and becoming another sad statistic. One of the smartest things you can do is read this book, learn about criminal law, and understand how to protect your rights.

Now, let's jump right in and start at the beginning. To understand the ins and outs of criminal law, you first have to understand what a crime is and what makes you a criminal. Simply put, it is a crime to break a government rule. And, breaking a government rule makes you a criminal. That's all it takes. You don't have to be a bad person and you don't always have to intend to cause something bad to happen. We repeat, you break a government rule and you can be branded a criminal. Got it? Good. That's one definition of a criminal. But, let's dig a little deeper.

Here's another way to define what makes you a criminal: you commit a crime whenever you do something that causes a certain result the government does not want to see. We'll call such a result a "criminal result" throughout this book. For example, the government does not want to see people end up dead from gun shots. The government has a rule stating that people can't just bust guns and shoot other people. In other words, they outlaw murder. If you were to take a gun, shoot, and kill somebody in cold blood, you would have committed the crime of murder. The shooting caused the criminal result—a person ending up dead from gun shots. YOU would be a criminal because you caused that result that the government did not want to see.

Laws

A government rule is better known as a "law," so that's what we'll call government rules from now on. There are pages and pages of laws written by the federal, state, and local governments. Laws cover everything from the most well-known crimes, like murder and armed robbery, down to the most unfamiliar crimes like cussin' in front of women and children. Laws usually make sense based on what people think is right and wrong, but sometimes it seems as though they're made just to hassle people. No matter what you think about the laws, you have to follow them. Remember, not following the law is what makes you a criminal.

Why have laws? Well, governments write laws to "keep order" and to "protect" citizens. For example, if the government didn't make it illegal to steal, anybody bigger or stronger than you could punk you and take your stuff at any time. Or how about when you're driving? You need to know that when you turn the corner in your new, freshly-shined Cadillac Escalade there won't be some fool driving head-on toward you. The government requires everybody to drive on the right side of the road. Laws make it easier and safer to drive. Ultimately, laws make it easier and safer to live.

Punishment

Laws are only helpful when people follow them, so if you break a law, the government punishes you. Sometimes they throw you in jail. Other times they make you pay money or put restrictions on you, or take away privileges they give to you. For instance, they might suspend your driver's license. Yeah, that's what happened to your friend's daddy when he got caught drunk driving or "DUI". These punishments are expected to discourage you from breaking the laws, which should result in everybody living in a safer environment. But, you can be the judge of how much safer it is where you live because of the laws you are expected to follow.

PART I:

CRIMES, THUGGIN', AND CRIMINAL OFFENSES

CHAPTER I:

WHERE YOUR HEAD IS AT WHEN A CRIME IS COMMITTED

Section A: Committing Crimes On Purpose

We told you in the Introduction that you don't always have to intend to cause a criminal result in order to be branded a criminal. Luckily, most times you *do* have to cause a criminal result on purpose in order to be convicted. Take this example: Jon-Jon wants Malcolm's 28-inch chrome rims and decides to steal them. He waits until three o'clock in the morning, goes over to Malcolm's apartment complex, and steals the rims off Malcolm's truck, leaving it on blocks. That's a pretty clear case of committing a crime on purpose. Jon-Jon wanted to do the crime and purposely did all the necessary stuff which made his actions the crime of stealing. Everybody understands that he did the crime on purpose.

The Law Says You Committed the Crime on Purpose, You Say You Didn't

Most times, if you didn't *intend* to do anything illegal, you won't get into trouble. In the example above, Jon-Jon intended to steal the rims and went through with it, so he'll be in big trouble when he gets caught. The problem is that there are a lot of funky situations where the government can say that you intended to commit a crime. Have you ever heard the phrase, "Knowing is half the battle"? Well, the government says that you purposely broke the law if you knew, or should have known that you were doing something criminal. The following example explains one way the government can say you committed a crime on purpose even if you claim you didn't.

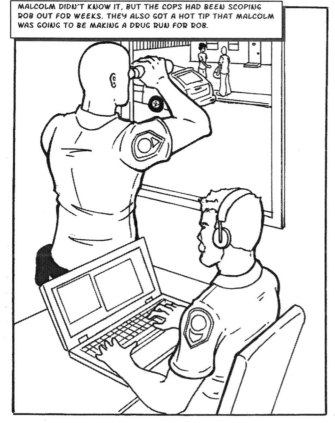

Guess what? Malcolm has just committed all kinds of drug trafficking crimes like 1) possession with intent to distribute, 2) conspiracy (we'll explain conspiracy in detail later because the crime of conspiracy is how you really get messed up by the prosecution), 3) carrying illegal drugs across state lines, and the list goes on. The government will say that he did it all on purpose. Why? Because Malcolm *knew* Rob was a drug dealer who made that Tennessee run, even if he and Rob didn't talk about it. Malcolm did the run anyway because he wanted those two bills. Knowing what he did about the situation made that run an intentional attempt to transport drugs across state lines along with a bunch of other charges that the prosecutor will throw at him.

Everybody knows Malcolm freakin' knew what was up. And, the prosecutor and the jury are gonna be like, "Malcolm knew," and they are going to convict him for some major stuff, all over two bills! The moral of the story is that the law will say you purposely committed a crime whenever you knew enough about a situation that you should have known you were doing some illegal stuff.

Willful Blindness

But, what if Malcolm really didn't know anything about Rob being a drug dealer or that Tennessee run? And, what if Malcolm thought the run was a little suspect, but intentionally didn't ask any questions because he didn't want to find out if there was something illegal going on? Could Malcolm still be on the hook for drug trafficking? **HELL YES!** The law will use a rule called "willful blindness" to bust Malcolm even if he really didn't know what was up. Willful blindness is when you intentionally ignore facts, or refuse to find out info that would probably let you know that what you are doing is a crime. The law doesn't like willful blindness, so it assumes that you caused the criminal result on purpose, never mind what you *actually* knew about the situation.

TO RECAP

- You can't get over on the legal system by pretending that you didn't know you were breaking the law.
- The law will punish you for not finding out if you could be breaking the law.

Section B: Committing Crimes By Mistake

One of the main reasons that folks in the hood, especially young men, get caught out there is that they do too much risky stuff that could accidentally lead to the injury or death of other people—stuff like walking around with heat or speeding in cars. That's not to say that suburban guys don't do the same stuff. But, dudes in the hood usually can't afford good lawyers to get them off like suburban dudes can.

Reckless Conduct or Knucklehead-Type Crap Can Land You in the Slammer

Let's start with reckless conduct. Reckless conduct is whenever you do some risky stuff that you *know* is likely to hurt or kill somebody but you do it anyway because you just don't care. For instance, if you pull out a gun and shoot into a house you know is crowded, that's reckless. In fact, that's so reckless that if you hurt somebody it could land you a battery charge. That's because you know you're likely to hit somebody if you shoot into a crowded house. What's even worse is that if the person you hit dies, you could be on the hook for murder.

Criminal Negligence Crimes

Criminal negligence, is when you do some risky stuff that you *should have known* was likely to hurt or kill somebody, but you didn't actually know because it just didn't come to your mind. Here's an example to help you understand:

MALCOLM'S BABY'S MAMA, TAMIKA, THE SAME CHICK WHO'S ALWAYS IN HIS POCKETS FOR MONEY BUT WHO NEVER LETS HIM SEE HIS DAUGHTER, DECIDES SHE'S GONNA GO CLUBBIN' AFTER SHE PUTS THE KID TO SLEEP – NEVER MIND GETTING A BABYSITTER.

AFTER THE KID DOZES OFF, TAMIKA HEADS TO THE CLUB. . .

AND PROCEEDS TO DO HER THING ON THE DANCE FLOOR.

TAMIKA'S DAUGHTER WAKES UP IN THE MIDDLE OF THE NIGHT.

MAMA?

I'M HUNGRY

NOT SURPRISED THAT HER MOM'S NOT AROUND, (APPARENTLY, TAMIKA DOES THIS KIND OF THING ALL THE TIME) THE KID WALKS TO THE KITCHEN AND DECIDES TO BOIL SOME HOT DOGS. SHE'S SEEN HER MOM DO IT BEFORE AND THERE'S ALREADY A POT OF WATER ON THE STOVE.

ONCE THE WATER GETS GOOD AND HOT, THE KID TRIES TO PULL THE POT OFF THE STOVE BUT ACCIDENTALLY DROPS IT, SCALDING HERSELF IN THE PROCESS.

THE KID RUNS OUT THE FRONT DOOR SCREAMING FOR HER MAMA.

ONE OF THE NEIGHBORS HEARS HER AND CALLS 911.

TAMIKA NEEDS TO BE SMACKED FOR LEAVING HER DAUGHTER HOME ALONE, DOESN'T SHE? WELL, THE LAW WILL SMACK HER (FIGURATIVELY SPEAKING, OF COURSE). SHE'S GONNA GET ARRESTED AND HIT WITH SOME SORT OF CHILD ENDANGERMENT OR NEGLECT CHARGE.

Now, even though Tamika is a sorry excuse for a mom, if we could read her mind, we'd see that she really didn't know that her girl could get hurt. Still, she took a risk that most people know could lead to a kid getting hurt or killed when she left shorty home alone at night. Even though Tamika didn't actually know about the risk to her baby girl, she *should have known* better. She's criminally negligent. Unfortunately for Tamika, the kid probably gets taken away, *and* Tamika gets thrown in jail. Ignorance is no excuse.

TO RECAP
- If something bad happens while you are doing something that you definitely know is dangerous and likely to cause harm, you can be charged with a serious crime.
- If something bad happens while you are doing something that you should know is dangerous and could possibly cause harm, you could be charged with a crime.

Section C: If You Did it, You Committed a Crime, No Excuses

Being charged with a crime for doing something you should have known could lead to a crime is tough, but the government has something even tougher than that. You can be charged with a crime for breaking the law even though there was NO WAY IN HELL you could have or even should have known you were about to cause a criminal result. That's what happens when you commit what is called a strict liability crime.

A strict liability crime works like this. A law says don't do something. If you do it, you get charged. That's it. The government doesn't care whether you did it on purpose, did it accidentally, didn't know something bad would happen, should've known something bad could've happened, or just didn't care. Most people are familiar with the strict liability crime of statutory rape. Some people argue that statutory rape can end up being real bogus. Why? Because all a prosecutor has to do is prove that a guy over a certain age had sex with a pretty young thang under a certain age. It doesn't matter if the guy didn't really have any reason to think the girl was under the legal age. The fact that the girl is actually down with the get down doesn't mean jack. If the dude is of adult age—the girl is underage—and they screw, he's going to jail. She could have told him she was 30 years old. The man is still going to do serious time for statutory rape. He'll also have to register as a convicted sex offender. Registering as a sex offender means he will have a hard time finding a job and a place to live for the rest of his life. And, the same thing goes for a woman having sex with an under-aged boy.

In the meantime, some junior and senior high school boys are doing hard time for screwin' their freshman and sophomore girlfriends. What the hell is that about? At any rate, if you are a senior or junior having sex with a freshman or sophomore in high school, you might be running the risk of your girl's parents getting pissed and pressing charges against you for statutory rape once they find out you've been taggin' their baby every day after school while they're at work. And, don't do somethin' silly like get their baby girl pregnant. Why? Because it'll be real easy to prove you were sexin' daddy's little princess. A positive paternity test and the case is closed. Go straight to jail. Do not pass go.

TO RECAP

- Once you've done what it takes to commit a strict liability crime, it doesn't matter if you knew it was a crime or whether you tried to commit it. You can be charged with that crime.

CHAPTER 2

GETTIN' IN TROUBLE FOR DOING NOTHIN'

Section A. Not Doing Nothin', Generally

Did you know that you don't even have to do anything sometimes and you can still be charged with a crime? It's true. You can be charged, convicted, and sentenced for a crime without even moving a muscle. In fact, you can get in trouble with the law exactly for that reason—not moving a muscle. There are some crimes that are committed when you don't do something that you are supposed to do. These are crimes of omission. So you see, the government not only has rules in place to keep you from doing certain things, it also has rules in place to make sure you do certain things.

ONE DAY, MALCOLM ASKS HIS UNCLE RON TO GO HIKING IN THE MOUNTAINS WITH HIM.

HEY UNCLE RON, WHAT DO YOU SAY YOU AND I GO FOR A HIKE IN THE MOUNTAINS?

SURE YOUNG BUCK, I'LL GO HIKING WITH YOU.

THEY HEAD ON UP THE MOUNTAIN REACHING THE TOP WITH NO PROBLEMS. AFTER CHECKING OUT THE VIEW FOR A WHILE, THEY HEAD DOWN.

ABOUT HALFWAY DOWN THE MOUNTAIN MALCOLM STUMBLES OVER A FALLEN BRANCH AND HURTS HIMSELF.

UNCLE RON SEES MALCOLM GO DOWN AND LAUGHS

DANG, MAN, YOU IS ONE CLUMSY DUDE!

UNCLE RON KEEPS WALKING BACK HOME. MALCOLM WOULD'VE SURVIVED IF UNCLE RON HAD HELPED HIM BACK TO THE CITY, BUT SINCE UNCLE RON DECIDED TO LAUGH AT HIM RATHER THAN HELP HIM, MALCOLM ENDS UP BLEEDING TO DEATH.

Uncle Ron might be charged with a crime for Malcolm's death since he didn't help Malcom out when Malcom was in trouble. Sure, Malcolm was clumsy, and Uncle Ron had nothing at all to do with him falling over that branch. Hell, the hiking trip was Malcolm's dumb idea anyway. He even refused to pack the communication radio that Uncle Ron told him to before they headed out that morning. But, Uncle Ron could still be brought up on criminal charges for *not* helping Malcolm out once the situation requiring his help came up.

See, Malcolm and Uncle Ron went hiking together, and Uncle Ron is supposed to look out for his nephew in a situation like that. Malcolm is his fam and Uncle Ron is the adult responsible for Malcolm in that situation. Malcolm knows that and Uncle Ron knows that, and oddly enough, the law actually has a touch of morality and decency to it too. Since young Malcolm went on this hike with his grown-up Uncle Ron who is supposed to be looking after Malcolm, the prosecutor will legally slap Uncle Ron for leaving Malcolm hanging like that on the mountain. Honestly, he needs to go to jail for leaving his nephew on the mountain with a broke, bleedin' leg.

Another situation where you can get in trouble for not doing anything is if you start to help somebody who's in danger. In some situations, if you start to help somebody who's in serious danger, you have to see things through to the end or otherwise end up in serious trouble. Take this next example.

ONE NIGHT CARLOS AND ZEB DECIDE TO HIT THE STREETS AND CLUB HOP. BECAUSE THEY AIN'T EVER TRYIN' TO BLOW ALL THEIR CASH AT THE BAR, THEY USUALLY STOP BY THE LIQUOR STORE TO PICK UP A STARTER BEVERAGE OR TWO BEFORE GOING INSIDE THE CLUB.

AFTER HITTING THE LIQUOR STORE, THE GUYS GO TO ZEB'S CAR TO SIP FOR AWHILE. THEY PLAN ON DRINKING JUST ENOUGH TO GET A NICE BUZZ.

AFTER ABOUT 20 MINUTES, CARLOS GETS ANXIOUS BECAUSE HE SPOTS TWO FINE LADIES WALKING INTO THE BAR

YO, YOU SEE THEM? FINISH THAT DRINK SO WE CAN GO IN AND HOLLA!

CARLOS AND ZEB QUICKLY DOWN THEIR DRINKS AND WALK INTO THE CLUB. ONCE INSIDE, CARLOS SPOTS THE CHICKS AND POINTS THEM OUT TO ZEB.

THERE THEY GO, OVER THERE IN THE CORNER!

WASTING NO TIME, CARLOS AND ZEB WALK OVER TO TALK TO THE LADIES BECAUSE THEY KNOW HOW IT CAN GET IN THE SPOT. WAIT TOO LONG AND SOME CRAB DUDES MIGHT SLIDE UP AND START CLINGING TO THE GIRLS WITH NO PLANS OF GIVING THEM ROOM TO BREATHE FOR THE REST OF THE NIGHT.

THE GUYS LAY THEIR TALK GAME DOWN AND THE LADIES ARE ALL IN. THE LADIES AND GUYS GET A BOOTH AND ALMOST IMMEDIATELY CARLOS AND ZEB GO OUT LIKE SUCKERS AND BREAK THEIR OWN RULE ABOUT NOT BUYING ALCOHOL AT THE CLUB. THEY OPEN A TAB AND THE BOTTLE POPPIN' JUMPS ALL NIGHT LONG.

NEXT MORNING, CARLOS IS WALKING BACK TO THE CAR WITH AN EAR-TO-EAR GRIN.

NEARING THE SPOT WHERE HE LEFT ZEB AND THE CAR, HE SEES SEVERAL POLICE CARS AND AN AMBULANCE. HIS SMILE QUICKLY FADES AND HE RUNS TOWARD ZEB'S CAR TO SEE IF EVERYTHING IS OKAY.

BUT EVERYTHING IS NOT OKAY. CARLOS TELLS THE COPS WHO HE IS AND ASKS WHAT HAPPENED. THEY TELL HIM THAT ZEB DIED IN THE CAR OVERNIGHT OF DEHYDRATION.

CARLOS MENTIONS HOW BAD HE FEELS ABOUT HANGING UP ON THE 911 DISPATCHER. HEARING THAT, THE COPS ARREST CARLOS FOR NOT FOLLOWING THROUGH WITH THE 911 CALL KNOWING THAT HIS BOY WAS IN SERIOUS DANGER.

Carlos is going to be in trouble because he started helping Zeb but then stopped. If he had followed through, Zeb might've lived. Once Carlos started helping Zeb, he had a duty to see things through and stay on the line with the 911 dispatch, which in turn could have possibly saved Zeb's life.

Section B: When Do You Have to Do Something?

The two examples above sound a little crazy, right? Outside of common decency, most people don't think that they have an obligation to help others. After all, there are tons of stories about people standing around doing nothing while somebody drowned or got beat up or even raped. Those bystanders didn't get in trouble. So, you think, "I really don't have to help anybody out of a dangerous situation if I don't want to." Ding, ding, ding, you're almost right. Most times you're perfectly free to be a jerk and not help somebody out when they're in danger. It all depends on whether you have a duty to help the person, which in turn depends on the situation itself, or whether a law requires you to help the person. Here's a list of rules that explain when you have a duty to help another person in danger:

- Status Relationships: Parents and older family members gotta help their children and younger family members. Husbands and wives must help each other and even bosses and employees gotta stick together. If your mean slave-driver of a boss is choking on some food and you don't pound him on the back to knock that crap out, you could be in trouble. Go ahead, you know you wanna pound him on the back anyway. Here's your free chance.

- A Law Says So: Many states have laws that require people involved in a car accident to help other people injured in the accident. Some states have laws that say club owners have to provide safety instructions to the people who go to their clubs to kick it. Some places have what are called, "Good Samaritan" laws, that say you even have to help strangers if you see them in need. So, in those places, you can be charged for a crime whenever you leave somebody hangin', even if you don't have a relationship with them.

- Contractual Obligations: Home nurses have to help the elderly people they're being paid to take care of. Lifeguards have to help swimmers at the beaches and pools they watch. Baby sitters gotta help the children they babysit. Boy Scout troop leaders gotta help the scouts. It's their job to help their clients or customers or people that they are supervising. Here, failure to do your job could mean more than getting fired. It could mean some serious jail time.

- You Caused the Problem in the First Place: If you do something to somebody, even a complete stranger, that puts them in a dangerous situation, you better help them out of it or you're through!

- You Got Involved and Tried to Help Somebody in Danger: If you find somebody in danger, danger that you didn't even cause, and you start to help them, you have to keep on helping or you could be setting yourself up for some serious trouble. Once you start to help somebody out, you can't leave them hangin' if you get tired or it turns out to be more of a hassle than you bargained for. The law says you can't leave somebody worse off than when you found them once you start helping them. Unless you are a certified doctor (and even doctors can get it wrong), you shouldn't gamble on your ability to tell if somebody is better or worse off than you found them once you've started helping. Stay until the authorities arrive or until there is absolutely no doubt they are okay. After you jump in there to be a hero, you have to see it through to the finish line homie.

TO RECAP

- You can commit a crime by not helping somebody when you should.
- Whether you can be charged with a crime for not helping somebody usually depends upon your relationship with the person.

CHAPTER 3:

CRIMINAL OFFENSES

The average person usually doesn't know what makes something a burglary, a robbery, or an assault. In other words, they don't know the elements of certain crimes. As a result, they often end up on the hook for somethin' they can't even explain. This chapter explains how the law defines certain crimes. We'll jump it off with the basic crimes against other people's property and move through until we get to the heavier stuff like murder.

Section A: Taking People's Property

Taking other folks' property is one of the oldest criminal acts on the books. They used to cut people's hands off for it back in Biblical days. Taking some stuff that didn't belong to you was highly frowned upon back then, and the government still ain't feelin' it today. Think about it, when you steal from somebody, you take somebody else's hard-earned stuff. Even if it wasn't earned the hard way, you are taking something that you don't have any right to have. What the heck makes you think you can just take people's stuff? But, that's a little off track ... getting back to stealing. There are 4 main ways you can commit the crime of stealing. You can commit 1) larceny, 2) embezzlement, 3) robbery and 4) burglary.

Larceny

Larceny is stealing the good old fashion way. When somebody grabs someone else's stuff and takes it away with the intent to keep it, that's larceny.

Some people think that you can't be charged with larceny of store items (shoplifting) until you've actually walked out of the store with the goods. WRONG! As soon as you pick up those items with the intent to steal them, and walk a few inches from where you got them, the law says you have carried the items away. Even if you have a change of heart and try to put the stuff back, you can still be hit with larceny.

Embezzlement

Embezzlement is the stuff you hear about on TV and it sounds complicated, but it really isn't. Basically, embezzlement is when you are given somebody else's property to hold rightfully, but you later decide you are going to make it yours wrongfully. The most common victims of embezzlement are employers. You know those sweet hookups your mama keeps getting from the job? Yeah, that's stuff she embezzled. The extra flat screen monitor that ended up hooked up to your home computer she got when she was ordering upgrades for the people in her office; the gas she puts in all the cars at the house with her job's gas card; or the printer paper she supposedly took home for printing up work at the house, but instead only uses it so you can print up stuff off the Internet; all that stuff is embezzled property. She works for her employer, so she is authorized to place orders for the office because it's part of her job. They may have given her a gas card because her job requires her to travel a lot. In order to work from home she may need to print stuff there, so her employer allows her to take printer paper home for that purpose. But, when she makes that stuff hers by using it for her own personal purposes, she's embezzling.

In a way, dope boys embezzle all the time. Every hood has that one dope boy who always has an excuse about why the dough came back short this time, or why the dope is a little lighter than last time. It's usually some stupid excuse like, "My supplier charged me more this time dawg, that ten grand only covered half of what it did the last time." You know like we know, if the dope was lighter it's because he was trimming it, and if the change was short it was because he was pocketing some of the cash. He's an embezzling jerk! If he's in the room while you're reading this, slap him right now and tell him that foul crap he does with the weight is called "embezzlement."

Robbery

Robbery is when somebody takes somebody else's stuff off the person or in front of the person by force or threat of harm with intentions to keep it forever. The perp doesn't even have to threaten the person he's robbing. The threat of harm could even be made against somebody with the person being robbed. For instance, a robber might run up on a father and son walking home. If he points the gun at the son while telling the father to "Run that watch or the kid gets it," he'd still be robbing the father. Another example of robbery is when some ignorant fool runs into a gas station, pulls out a gun and tells the person working the register to give him all $62 in the cash register. (Quick note: Robbing a gas station or convenience store is the DUMBEST THING you can do to try to make a buck. The register probably has less than $100 at any given time. You could face 20 years to life over less than $100! You would be better off selling your gun. It's probably worth more than the loot you will find in the register.) Some other examples of robbery follow:

A BULLY GOES UP TO A KID IN THE SCHOOL YARD AND TELLS HIM TO FORK OVER HIS LUNCH MONEY OR ELSE TAKE A POUNDIN'.

A THUG ROLLS UP ON A STORE CASHIER, PULLS OUT A GUN AND ORDERS HER TO EMPTY THE REGISTER.

26

Burglary

Burglary is when somebody illegally or without proper permission goes into a building with the purpose of committing a crime inside (usually stealing). If the building is open to the general public at the time you enter to commit your crime, or you have actual permission to be in the place, it's not burglary. If you go ahead and commit the crime you had planned when you entered, you will be charged for that particular crime, but not burglary.

If you read the explanation of burglary closely, you can see you don't have to actually "break" into a place to commit burglary. You don't have to throw a brick through the back window and climb through. You don't have to do anything dramatic like blow up the lock on the building with explosives. The door or window you go through to enter the building could even be unlocked and wide open. It doesn't matter. All you have to do is go into a building without permission with the intent to commit a crime inside. As soon as you enter without permission with the intent to commit a crime inside, it doesn't matter if you decide not to go ahead and commit the crime inside, you've already committed burglary. The crime of burglary is complete once you enter a building without permission with the intent to do somethin' foul like stealing stuff inside. If you're wondering how the authorities can tell that you intended to commit a crime while inside, most times the government assumes you intended to do a crime based purely on the fact that you broke in. This makes sense because most people don't break into places unless they intend to commit a crime inside.

TO RECAP

- Larceny is taking away somebody else's stuff without their permission with the intent to never give it back.
- Embezzlement is when somebody gives you something to use for them but you use the stuff for yourself even though you're not supposed to.
- Robbery is when you take somebody's stuff from them with the intent to never give it back by threatening to immediately hurt them, a loved one, or somebody close to them.
- Burglary is when you go into a building without permission with the intent to commit a crime inside.

Section B: Crimes Against Somebody's Body

Assault and Battery

On television, you hear the terms "assault" and "battery" thrown together almost every time somebody gets charged for whuppin' on somebody else. The problem is that it may confuse you as to what assault means and what battery means. Assault is a crime separate and completely different from battery.

Battery

Battery is the simplest of the two crimes to explain, so we'll begin with it. Battery is when you apply force to somebody else without their permission and it results in unwanted contact or injury to them. Obviously when you attack somebody without justification, you commit a battery. Also, when you touch that girl's fat booty when she walks by, you're committing a battery if she doesn't like it. This is true even if you are vibin' with a young lady on the dance floor, grinding and smiling in each other's face and you reach down and grab her butt in the moment. It could turn out that she felt like you went too far. Any unwanted physical contact with somebody else is a battery, so make sure that she wants you touching her before you get all close.

You can also be charged with battery for touching something connected to a person. For example, when you smack something out of somebody's hand, that's considered a battery. It's also a battery to do something like pull a chair from under somebody as they are about to sit in it.

It should go without saying that if you use something to wrongfully touch a person, that's battery too. For instance, if you stab somebody, or hit them with a bat, that's a battery. In fact, whenever you bring some outside tool like a knife or a bat into the mix, the crime becomes aggravated battery. Why is this important? Because the punishment for aggravated battery is worse than for a plain old battery. By the way, putting your nasty stank sock on another kid in gym class is also a battery, so watch them jokes.

BATTERY IS WHEN YOU TOUCH SOMEBODY IN A WAY THAT OFFENDS THEM OR WHEN THEY DON'T WANT YOU TO. AN EXAMPLE OF THIS IS WHEN YOU PUNCH SOMEBODY WITHOUT JUSTIFICATION.

Assault

Assault can be committed two different ways. The first way to commit an assault is to attempt to commit a battery on somebody. If you swing a bat at somebody and miss, that's an assault. The second way to commit an assault is to intentionally make somebody feel like you are going to physically hurt them right then and there. If you jump at somebody with raised shoulders and arms like you are going to blow their chest out, you commit an assault. But, the person has to be aware of the assault. If you do it behind the person's back, you won't be charged with an assault.

If Carlos gets up in his girlfriend Rita's face with his pimp hand ready, screaming at her about how he is going to break her neck for sleeping with his boy Malcolm, that's an assault. If Rita grabs a butcher knife from the kitchen and runs toward Carlos swearing up and down that she is going to cut him 'cause she saw him with that dirty skank, Bunny, she could be charged with assault. And, just like with battery, when extras (weapons and dangerous objects) are part of the assault—like Rita's knife in the previous example—the assault becomes aggravated assault. You know what that means. Rita's punishment will be worse than if she was only convicted for simple assault.

ASSAULT IS WHEN YOU TRY TO COMMIT A BATTERY ON SOMEBODY. FOR INSTANCE, IF YOU TAKE A SWING AT A GUY WITHOUT JUSTIFICATION AND MISS, YOU'VE ASSAULTED THE GUY.

ASSAULT IS ALSO WHEN YOU MAKE SOMEBODY THINK THAT YOU'RE GONNA CAUSE HIM IMMEDIATE HARM.

TO RECAP

- Battery is when you touch somebody when they don't want you to or in a way that offends them.
- Using weapons to commit a battery is aggravated battery and carries a heavier sentence than regular battery.
- Assault is when you try to commit a battery on somebody.
- Assault is also when you make somebody think that you're gonna cause them immediate harm.
- Using weapons to commit an assault is aggravated assault and carries a heavier sentence than regular assault.

Section C: Homicides & Murder

A homicide is defined as "a killing of one human being by another person." There are a lot of different times and ways people kill other people. Sometimes a homicide is a crime and sometimes it isn't. For now, we are going to discuss the homicides that are crimes and how you may be charged with a crime for committing a homicide.

Murder

Murder is the most infamous of the homicide crimes. A homicide is murder in the following four situations:

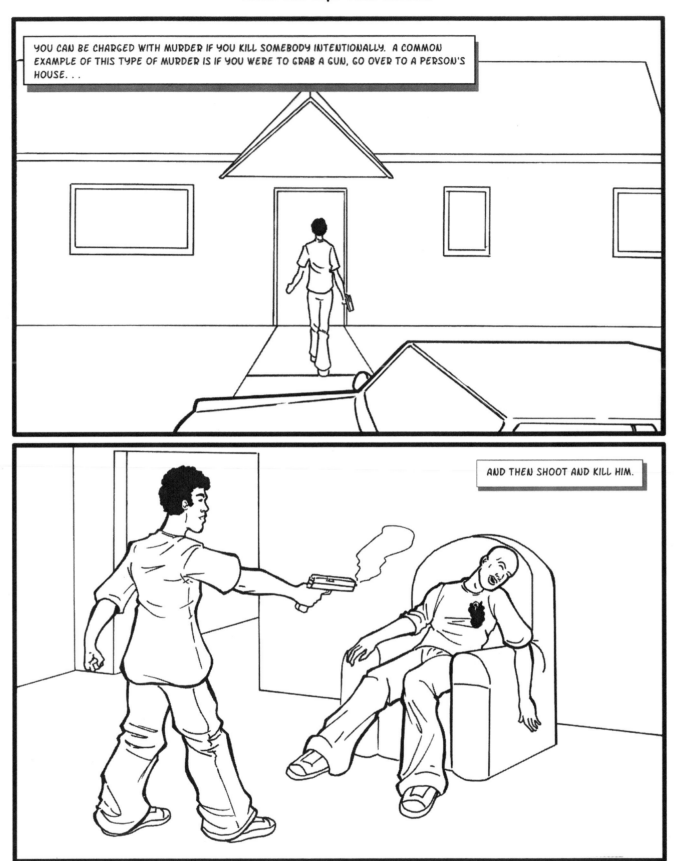

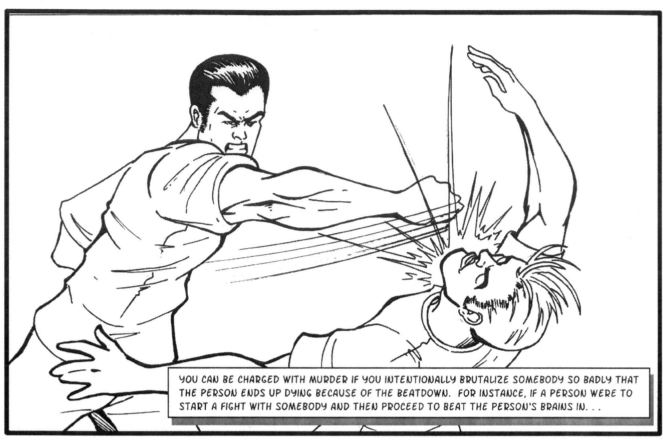

YOU CAN BE CHARGED WITH MURDER IF YOU INTENTIONALLY BRUTALIZE SOMEBODY SO BADLY THAT THE PERSON ENDS UP DYING BECAUSE OF THE BEATDOWN. FOR INSTANCE, IF A PERSON WERE TO START A FIGHT WITH SOMEBODY AND THEN PROCEED TO BEAT THE PERSON'S BRAINS IN. . .

HE COULD BE ON THE HOOK FOR MURDER IF THE PERSON HE BEAT UP DIES

YOU CAN BE CHARGED WITH MURDER FOR DOING SOMETHING THAT YOU KNOW WOULD LIKELY LEAD TO SOMEBODY'S DEATH BUT YOU DO IT ANYWAY AND A PERSON DIES BECAUSE OF WHAT YOU DID.

AN EXAMPLE OF THIS IS WHEN A FAKE GANGSTER PULLS OUT A PISTOL INSIDE A HOUSE PARTY, SHOOTS IT UP INTO THE AIR. . .

AND THE BULLET FROM THE GUN RICOCHETS OF THE CEILING. . .

AND STRAIGHT INTO THE HEART OF ONE OF HIS FAKE GANGSTA HOMIES, KILLING HIM IN THE PROCESS.

Voluntary Manslaughter

Voluntary Manslaughter is when you intentionally kill somebody because you are seriously provoked to do it and lose control before you have time to cool off. For example, if you walked in on your wife in bed with some other guy, you might be provoked to kill her and him.

Some people call voluntary manslaughter a "heat of passion" killing. In other words, you were so shocked and got heated so quick that you couldn't even think straight—you just straight "lost it." Normally you'd get charged with murder but because you were provoked, the crime gets knocked down to voluntary manslaughter. The good news is that you'll probably get a lighter sentence than if you were convicted for murder and you won't have to worry about the death penalty. But, don't get it twisted. You're still going to prison for a long time.

You might be thinking, "All right, anytime somebody sets me off I can kill that fool and only get a voluntary manslaughter charge." Not so fast, playa, it ain't quite that simple. In order to get a voluntary manslaughter charge instead of a murder charge, you have to have been seriously provoked. Simple words don't cut it! Just because somebody tells you they're gonna kick your butt, rape your girlfriend, or kidnap your children, it doesn't mean you've been seriously provoked. Walking in on your wife getting banged out by your best friend, that might do it, but keep in mind, in many places this law is changing so that walking in on your wife screwing around won't even do the trick anymore. And, really, you shouldn't even mess around with that. Like we said before, you still go to jail for voluntary manslaughter.

At any rate, you should know that the law looks at the following four elements, and they all have to be present to drop a murder charge down to voluntary manslaughter:

- First, you have to be suddenly provoked by something that would make the average person lose it; like unexpectingly finding your wife in bed with some other dude.

- Second, you have to actually be provoked. This means if somethin' wild suddenly happens to you but it doesn't actually cause you to lose your mind, you'll get hit with a murder charge.

- Third, there can't be enough time for the average person to cool down and get himself together. This means that if there was enough time for the average person in the same situation to cool down, the killing would be murder, even if YOU couldn't get YOUR temper under control. To say it again a little differently, the court will look at what happened and ask, "Would the average person have cooled down between the time he was provoked and the time he killed those fools?" How long does it take for the average person to cool down? Who knows? It's all up to the court to decide. Some courts might say the average person could've cooled down in five seconds. Some might say an hour or longer.

- Lastly, you can't cool down and get yourself together. If you did cool down, even for a moment before you killed your cheatin' wife and ol' dude, the killing will be murder. And, this is true even if the average person wouldn't have been able to cool down. It's all about you and whether you actually cooled down.

Involuntary Manslaughter

Involuntary Manslaughter is the next step down from voluntary manslaughter. There are two types of involuntary manslaughter. The first is a killing that results from doing something risky that you should have known could result in harm to a victim. The law sometimes calls this type of involuntary manslaughter "criminally negligent manslaughter." The second is when somebody gets killed during the commission of a crime that is not a dangerous felony. The law sometimes calls this type of involuntary manslaughter "unlawful act manslaughter" or "misdemeanor manslaughter."

Criminally negligent manslaughter happens when the perpetrator does something he should know is risky or does something with much less care than the average person would, and somebody ends up dead because of it.

MALCOLM IS DRIVING HIS CAR LATE ONE NIGHT.

HE DECIDES TO CHANGE THE RADIO STATION THAT HE'S LISTENING TO. AS HE'S FUMBLING WITH THE TUNER, HE ISN'T PAYING ATTENTION TO THE ROAD OR HIS DRIVING.

SUDDENLY, HE HEARS A LOUD THUMP AND LOOKS UP!

AND SEES THE FRONT END OF HIS CAR PLOWING INTO AND KILLING A HOMELESS GUY WHO WAS CROSSING THE STREET.

Malcolm's crime will not be murder or voluntary manslaughter here because he didn't kill the man on purpose. Still, Malcolm will have to pay the price for being less careful than everybody else would have been in the situation. Malcolm will be charged with criminally negligent manslaughter.

41

Unlawful act manslaughter usually happens when the perpetrator commits a misdemeanor or a nondangerous felony, and somebody gets killed in the process.

MALCOLM GETS A SLINGSHOT FOR CHRISTMAS. HE WANTS TO TEST IT OUT...

SO HE STANDS OUT IN HIS FRONT YARD AND TAKES A FEW SHOTS AT HIS NEIGHBOR'S GHETTO WIND CHIMES MADE OF SODA BOTTLES TIED TOGETHER. HE HITS ONE DEAD ON.

STARTLED BY THE SOUND OF SHATTERING GLASS,

MALCOLM'S NEIGHBOR GETS OUT OF HIS ROCKING CHAIR TO SEE WHAT'S GOING ON.

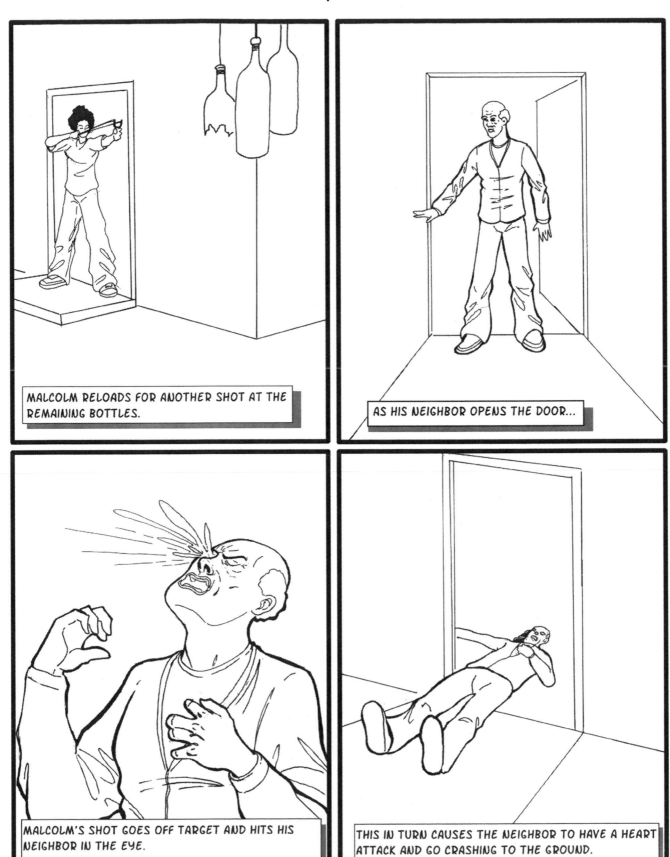

Here, Malcolm had no intention of killing his neighbor. But, Malcolm was intentionally shooting rocks with his slingshot at his neighbor's wind chime, and that's the crime of "destruction of property," which is a misdemeanor. Unfortunately, Malcolm killed his neighbor in the process of destroying the property and will likely be charged with unlawful act manslaughter, also referred to as misdemeanor manslaughter, the second form of involuntary manslaughter.

Homicide crimes are serious business and almost always get you some serious prison time. If the fact that killing another person is morally wrong doesn't stop you from committing a homicide crime, maybe the fact that you could spend a large chunk of your life behind bars will make you think twice. And, when you get out of the pen, most businesses won't hire ex-cons who did time for homicide.

TO RECAP
- Homicide is when you kill another person.
- You can be charged for murder if you kill somebody: 1) on purpose, 2) by inflicting serious bodily harm on them, 3) by your reckless actions or 4) during the commission of a dangerous felony.
- You can be charged for a homicide crime less serious than murder if you kill somebody accidentally or during the commission of a misdemeanor.

Section D: Early Stage & Incomplete Crimes

The three crimes that we are gonna talk about next are the ones that get the slickest of thugs caught up. Why do these crimes get the slickest of thugs? Because you can be arrested and convicted in the early stages of doing dirt. With these crimes, you only have to plan a crime or begin doing something illegal and you'll be going to jail as if you went through with the crime. These three crimes are 1) solicitation—soliciting criminal activity, 2) attempt—attempting criminal activity, and 3) conspiracy—conspiring to commit criminal activity. Many of your favorite gangsters have been caught because of conspiracy. Conspiracy is that real deal drama!

Solicitation

Let's start with the crime of solicitation. Imagine that Carlos has come up with a foolproof way to break into some guy's car and steal his stereo and speakers, but he wants somebody else to do it so he doesn't risk getting caught himself. He tells his friend, Juan, about the plan, asks him to do it and tells him that he can have the guy's amplifier if he decides to do it since that's all Juan needs to complete his own car sound system.

Well, without doing anything else, Carlos has just committed a crime. That's right, before they even pick a day for Juan to go out and steal the stuff, Carlos can be charged with solicitation. Hell, even before Juan gives him an answer about the heist, Carlos has committed the crime of solicitation. In short, if you ask, encourage, hire or command somebody to commit a crime, you have committed the crime of solicitation, and can do time for it.

Solicitation is one of the easiest crimes anybody can ever commit and it only takes a second to commit it. You probably have committed solicitation yourself and didn't even know it. Let's test the theory. Have you ever walked up to the register at your local McDonald's, saw your homegirl working and asked if she could "hook you up" with some free fries or an extra chicken sandwich. When you asked for the hookup, the moment that came out of your mouth, you committed the crime of solicitation. Your girl didn't have to say yes, she didn't even have to actually hear you. All it took was you asking for the "hook up" within ear shot. Getting down to it, when you ask somebody to "hook you up," you are asking them to steal those items or at least help you steal those items from the people you are supposed to be paying for them. Stealing is a crime, and asking somebody to help you steal is the crime of solicitation.

Attempt

It is a crime to try to commit a crime. For example, trying to steal some money is a crime even if you don't get the money. Trying to kill somebody by putting antifreeze in their food is a crime even if they don't actually eat the food and die. Trying to commit a crime is the crime of attempt. A lot of things count as attempting to commit a crime. You can be charged with attempting to commit a crime by doing things such as planning for it, talking to people whose help you'll need to carry it out, gathering materials to do it, and things like that.

Just so there's no confusion as to what types of things are considered attempting to commit a crime, let us give you a couple more examples. First we'll give you an example of something that is a clear attempt to commit a crime. Then we'll give you a variation that you may not have thought would count as an attempt to commit a crime.

SUDDENLY OUT OF NOWHERE, MALCOLM IS SURROUNDED BY THE COPS. THEY YELL AT HIM TO GET HIS SORRY BUTT OUT OF THE VEHICLE.

THEY THEN HANDCUFF AND ARREST HIM FOR ATTEMPTED ARMED ROBBERY.

BUT I DIDN'T EVEN GO IN! HOW COULD I ATTEMPT TO ROB THE BANK IF I DIDN'T GO IN?!

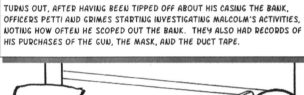

TURNS OUT, AFTER HAVING BEEN TIPPED OFF ABOUT HIS CASING THE BANK, OFFICERS PETTI AND GRIMES STARTING INVESTIGATING MALCOLM'S ACTIVITIES, NOTING HOW OFTEN HE SCOPED OUT THE BANK. THEY ALSO HAD RECORDS OF HIS PURCHASES OF THE GUN, THE MASK, AND THE DUCT TAPE.

THEY PEEPED HIM LEAVING HIS HOUSE WITH ALL OF THAT STUFF IN HAND ON THE DAY OF THE PLANNED ROBBERY. TAILING HIM AT A DISTANCE, THEY PARKED AND WAITED. AT FIRST THEY WERE GOING TO NAB HIM AS HE GOT NEAR THE DOORS BUT NOTICED HIM TURNING BACK AND DECIDED TO ARREST HIM ONCE HE GOT INTO HIS CAR.

It won't matter that Malcolm didn't get any money. All that matters is that he tried to rob the place.

In the second example, there is a small chance it matters that Malcolm decided not to go through with the robbery and was headed home. But, don't forget, in court the judge and the jury are going to look at all that crap he did in preparation and think, "Malcolm is a good-for-nothing thug type dude" and they are likely to find him guilty of attempted robbery so they can lock him up away from society.

They might also think that just because Malcolm didn't go through with it that day doesn't mean he wouldn't go through with it tomorrow or some other day. The bottom line is this, once you start to do some stuff that is moving toward committing a crime, you are leaving yourself open to the mercy or punishment of a bunch of people that don't know you and may not even be trying to hear about how you changed your mind at the last minute. So, don't start none, won't be none!

Conspiracy

We know you've heard something about conspiracy before somewhere in your lifetime. Maybe it was your parents talking about the government conspiracy to do this or that. Or maybe it was from some mystery show on TV where the bad guys came up with some elaborate plan to take over the world. Well, we're here to tell you the real deal about conspiracy, and the first thing you need to know is that it is one of the best tools the police and the prosecution use to get people. The second thing you need to know about conspiracy is that it doesn't require the involvement of a mastermind or a complex plan.

To be charged with conspiracy, all you have to do is agree with at least one other person to commit a crime or to help commit a crime. Some states give you a little protection by saying that you have to at least attempt to do some part of the crime, like buy the supplies that you'll need for the crime or show up at the house you agreed to break into. But, there are some states where all you have to do is agree to commit the crime. You can go to jail for conspiracy just like that. The reason is that the government is very worried about groups of people agreeing to commit a crime. There is strength in numbers, so a group of people plotting a crime is more dangerous than one person, and that's why the law cracks down hard on conspiracies.

You should assume that the moment you agree with somebody to commit or help commit a crime, the cops and prosecution can nail you. Just imagine, you can be thrown in jail for conspiracy the moment one of your friends asks you to help commit a crime and you say, "No doubt, let's do it!" And, just in case you're wondering how the cops would know that you agreed to commit the crime, they just ask your homies who were involved (your co-defendants) after they catch them. Most times the other guys will say you agreed to commit the crime because the prosecution will promise them less prison time if they snitch on you.

To help you better understand how conspiracy works, we're going to give you two examples of conspiracy. In this first example, we have the following four people involved in the conspiracy: Malcolm, Carlos, Zeb and Rob. This first example is a long one, but it's an important one, so stay with it and peep the pictures to help you follow along.

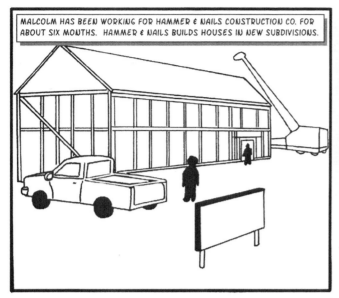

MALCOLM HAS BEEN WORKING FOR HAMMER & NAILS CONSTRUCTION CO. FOR ABOUT SIX MONTHS. HAMMER & NAILS BUILDS HOUSES IN NEW SUBDIVISIONS.

MALCOLM HAS KEYS TO A LOT OF THE HOUSES THAT ARE BEING CONSTRUCTED. HE ALSO HAS THE WORK SCHEDULE SO HE KNOWS WHEN HIS SUPERVISORS WON'T BE AROUND THE HOUSES.

SO HE COMES UP WITH A "BRILLIANT" IDEA TO MAKE SOME MONEY WHILE AT THE SAME TIME KEEPING SUSPICION OFF HIMSELF.

LISTEN, CARLOS, ALL YOU GOTTA DO IS GO INTO THE HOUSES AND SCOOP THE APPLIANCES OUT WHILE ME AND THE CONSTRUCTION CREW ARE WORKING AT A DIFFERENT SITE.

NO DOUBT! GIMME THE KEYS AND LET ME KNOW WHEN YOU AND THE CREW WON'T BE AROUND. MY BOY, ROB, CAN FENCE THE STUFF ON THE STREETS FOR US ONCE WE GET IT OUT.

CARLOS CALLS UP ZEB (BUT DOESN'T TELL MALCOLM THAT HE'S INVOLVING ZEB) TO HELP HIM GET THE STUFF.

I'M DOWN. JUST LET ME KNOW WHEN AND WHERE YOU WANNA MEET. I NEED A NEW DRYER FOR MY CRIB, ANYWAY

UNFORTUNATELY, THEY HAVE A "SMALL" PROBLEM.

YO, ZEB, I DON'T THINK MY TRUCK'S BIG ENOUGH TO HAUL THE STUFF.

NO PROBLEM, I KNOW WHAT TO DO.

53

SEE, MALCOLM'S SUPERVISOR THOUGHT MALCOLM WAS SHADY SINCE HIS FIRST DAY OF WORK. HE KEPT A CLOSE EYE ON MALCOLM AND SOMEHOW GOT WIND OF HIS PLAN

HE NOTIFIED OFFICERS GRIMES AND PETTI AND THEY SET UP CAMERAS IN THE TARGET HOUSES. AFTER WATCHING THE SURVEILLANCE TAPES FROM THE HOUSES AND SEEING CARLOS IN THEM THEY CAMP OUT AT ROB'S HOUSE WAITING FOR ZEB TO SHOW UP TO GIVE ROB THE STOLEN GOODS.

THEY KNEW THAT CARLOS WAS COOL WITH ROB, WHO THEY HAD ARRESTED BEFORE FOR SELLING STOLEN GOODS. ONCE ZEB SHOWS UP TO GIVE ROB THE STOLEN STUFF, OFFICERS GRIMES AND PETTI ARREST HIM AND ROB. AND THEY GET ARREST WARRANTS FOR MALCOLM AND CARLOS

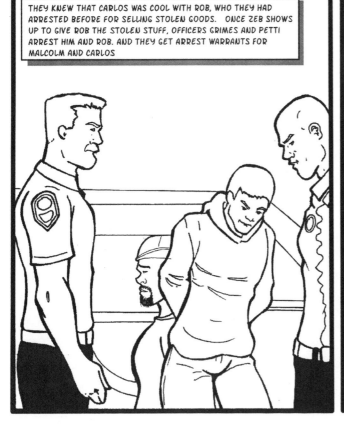

SO *EVERYBODY* INVOLVED EVENTUALLY GETS ARRESTED AND TAKEN TO THE STATION.

PLEASE PAY EXTRA CLOSE ATTENTION NOW. EVERY SINGLE PERSON CAUGHT UP IN A CONSPIRACY GETS CHARGED WITH THE CRIME OF CONSPIRACY (WHICH IS A CRIME ALL BY ITSELF), AND THEY ALSO GET CHARGED WITH EACH CRIME THAT WAS COMMITTED TO ACCOMPLISH THE GOAL OF THE CONSPIRACY. Malcolm, Carlos, Zeb and Rob will all be hit with conspiracy right off the jump. And, since Zeb stole the U-Haul to help accomplish the conspiracy, Carlos and Rob as well as Malcolm (who didn't even know Zeb was involved), will all get charged with grand theft auto too.

The thing about conspiracy is that the law considers your agreement to be involved as your agreement and participation in everything that has to be done to push the crime along. Once you're in, you're in all the way baby! If Zeb had straight carjacked somebody for the U-Haul and shot and killed him, Malcolm, Carlos and Rob could all be on the hook for that murder. The prosecutor is going to stack so many charges up on them they won't even be able to see over the top of them! And, you can bet that at least one of the charges is going to stick.

Conspiracy charges are used by the police and prosecution to make everybody who was even remotely involved look as responsible as the slimiest person involved. They charge everybody together, try everybody together if possible, and present evidence against everybody together. With that in mind, understand that the goal is to lump everything together against everybody, and to get YOU.

Here's another, less complicated example of conspiracy so you don't fall into that trap of thinking it takes a whole lot of players and a clever scheme to get tagged for it. In this conspiracy, the players are just Malcolm and Carlos.

MALCOLM HAS HAD BEEF WITH JON-JON SINCE LAST YEAR WHEN JON-JON TRIED TO HOLLER AT HIS GIRL, ASHLEY, AT THEIR HIGH SCHOOL GRADUATION PARTY. LIKE A PUNK, JON-JON TRIED TO PUSH UP ON ASHLEY WHILE MALCOLM WASN'T AROUND.

IT'S A YEAR LATER AND MALCOLM IS STILL KICKIN' IT WITH ASHLEY.

WANTING TO CHECK OUT HIS HOMEY CARLOS SKOOL SOME FOOLS ON THE COURT, MALCOLM AND ASHLEY ROLL UP TO ONE OF CARLOS' SUMMER BASKETBALL LEAGUE GAMES.

AS MALCOLM AND ASHLEY ARE GOING UP THE BLEACHERS TO FIND SOME SEATS, THAT FOOL, JON-JON, WHO'S SITTING ON THE BOTTOM ROW, TRIES TO GRAB ASHLEY'S ARM TO TALK TO HER—AS IF MALCOLM WASN'T RIGHT THERE WITH HER!

IT'S TIME TO CLAP THIS FOOL. HE GRABBED MY GIRL'S ARM IN FRONT OF ME LIKE I WAS A SUCKER OR SOMETHING.

JON-JON'S DISRESPECT GETS MALCOLM HEATED AND HE DECIDES THAT ENOUGH IS ENOUGH. AT HALFTIME, MALCOLM GOES INTO THE LOCKER ROOM TO LET CARLOS KNOW WHAT WENT DOWN.

YOU GONNA HELP ME OR WHAT?

YOU KNOW I GOT YOU. JUST WAIT UNTIL THE NEXT DEAD BALL SO I CAN GET MY BAT.

Now looking at Malcolm and Carlos' situation, you can easily see where the conspiracy came in. Malcolm asked Carlos to help whup Jon-Jon's tail and Carlos agreed. They proceeded to do what they agreed to do and beat the dog crap outta Jon-Jon. No long drawn out plan was required. Only two people were involved, and the crime was as simple as whupping somebody's butt. The twist is that Malcolm and Carlos didn't even agree to kill Jon-Jon. They simply agreed to beat him up. But, because there is evidence that supports an agreement to beat him up and they were doing it so brutally, if they go to trial, the jury will probably find that they agreed to kill Jon-Jon.

A note for you: if you agree with your boy to whup up on a Jon-Jon of your own, and your boy has plans to kill him instead, you may end up charged with murder if you start beating up Jon-Jon and your boy is successful in killing him. If you have ever agreed to mob out on somebody with a whole crew before, you may not have known it, but you were leaving yourself at the mercy of the personal whim of each member of your crew, including that real crazy idiot that ya'll can't ever calm down! Do you really wanna be leaving your freedom in the hands of that crazy bastard?

Dangers of Conspiracy

Beyond the simple fact that conspiracy itself is a crime, and you can be convicted and punished for it like any other crime, the charge of conspiracy is quite dangerous to anybody who is thinking about doing dirt. As we touched on earlier, you can be charged with multiple crimes committed to help move the conspiracy along. Even if you have a small unimportant part in a conspiracy you can end up doing hard time like some cold-hearted thug.

Take the previous example where Malcolm and the crew were stealing appliances from newly constructed homes. All those guys seem to be the kind of guys that might steal some stuff. They probably weren't really into hurting people physically. But, if Zeb had carjacked somebody and killed them in the process, all four of those dudes could be convicted as murderers. Now burglary and larceny are serious crimes, but they still don't compare to murder. It takes a particularly screwed up dude to murder somebody, especially over a U-Haul. All four of them could be convicted and sentenced as if all of them was that screwed up dude, just because one of them happened to be.

What's even more foul about this result is that the crazy killer is probably better able to do hard time because he will clearly mess somebody up if he feels like it, so you know he will handle his business in prison if he has to. But, the other three dudes are probably gonna end up somebody's prison babe because they'll be thrown in with cold hard killers while they're really just thieves. If they do happen to survive and thrive in a maximum security prison for hard killers, it's probably because they will have become hardened criminals over time instead of the nonviolent thieves that they were before they went inside.

Conspiracy charges can cause some really messed up results. Keep that big, burly, snarling, nasty fella with the tats all down his neck and arm who might become your cellmate in mind next time you're thinking about doin' somethin' stupid with somebody to come up.

Another common example of conspiracy charges ending in unfair results is when a girlfriend or a wife of a heavy dope pusher gets sentenced to jail for crazy years just for doing stuff like taking a couple of phone messages. Or she ends up getting years in prison for driving her man to a dope spot because it was on her way to the mall to pick up clothes for their baby. You may have heard about this type of stuff plenty of times but never really knew how it was that somebody who was not really that involved could get hit with serious prison time. Often they are getting convicted as if they were doing all the same stuff the heavy dealer was doing through a conspiracy charge. It usually goes down like this next example:

BECAUSE THEY KNOW WHAT'S UP WITH THE HOUSE, THEY ALSO KNOW WHEN MIKE IS IN THERE SLANGIN'. SO THEY RAID THE SPOT AND PICK UP EVERYBODY INSIDE, INCLUDING KEISHA.

PETTI AND GRIMES GO ALL THROUGH HER STUFF.

AND END UP FINDING SOME PHONE MESSAGES SHE WROTE DOWN WITH INSTRUCTIONS FOR MIKE FROM HIS DRUG CONTACT.

THAT WAS BAD ENOUGH, BUT WHAT KEISHA DIDN'T KNOW IS THAT THEY HAD PREVIOUSLY TAPED HER DRIVING MIKE TO ANOTHER DOPE SPOT AROUND THE WAY A COUPLE OF TIMES.

PLUS THEY SAW MIKE DROP HER A COUPLE HUNDRED DOLLAR BILLS (MONEY TO GET HER HAIR DONE, OR SOME NEW SHOES SHE'D BEEN WANTING) WHEN HE CAME BACK OUT OF THE OTHER DOPE SPOT.

The prosecutor charges Keisha with drug distribution through a conspiracy charge, and hits her with the weight that was found on Mike as if it was hers and she was the one out there slangin' it. Also, since she's a small timer who's barely involved at all, she doesn't have anybody to give up or rat on (like ol' boy in your 'hood who keeps getting tagged on Thursday but is back on the street before the weekend hits). She's gonna do time, while Mike is gonna cop a plea, snitch on some people, and be out kickin' it with that other chick who is always in his face whenever Keisha ain't around. Ladies, this can happen to you. If you are kickin' it with a thug, you may end up in jail because of somethin' he did. Stay away from the thugs unless you don't mind going to jail.

Accomplice Liability and Being Guilty for the Crimes of Other People
Have you ever heard the phrase, "guilty by association"? If you haven't, let us hip you to it real quick. The phrase means that you can be charged with a crime by being associated with somebody who has committed a crime. Unlike conspiracy, you don't have to agree to be part of the crime at all. All you have to do is help the perpetrator in some way. The legal system calls this type of liability "accomplice liability." You are an accomplice if you 1) help somebody get ready to commit a crime, 2) help them while they're in the process of committing a crime, or 3) help them escape or avoid being caught right after they've committed a crime.

The law can find that you have helped somebody commit a crime in a lot of different ways. See, most people understand that they have helped a robber commit a robbery by giving him a 9-mm handgun to rob a convenience store. Most people know they are helping a perpetrator by filling a bag with money from the register while the perpetrator holds a gun to a convenience store owner's head screaming, "Don't move or I'll blow your friggin head off!" Also, most folks know that they would be helping to commit a crime if they sit outside in the driver's side of a getaway car waiting for the robbers to come running out so they can speed off to a safe location. But, what most people don't know is that accomplice liability allows you to get tagged for all kinds of small-type stuff too.

Did you know that you can be found guilty as an accomplice to a murder for hyping up the murderer before the crime? For example, if you drive a friend around the neighborhood for a while hyping him up to go smoke somebody you can be convicted as an accomplice to murder if he actually does go smoke somebody. You can be charged with a crime as an accomplice just by being there while it was happening if a court can find that you were there to offer help if needed. This is the case even if you never end up helping at all. Or if a fight breaks out at the club, and you stand around while the winner is pounding the loser's face and you're cheering him on to, "Kill 'em," you can end up on the hook as an accomplice to battery or murder if he actually listens to you and goes ahead and kills the dude.

All you "ride-or-die" chicks out there, you can be on the hook for whatever gangsta stuff your man does if you let him come lay low at your house after he's been out thuggin'. Yep, you can be considered an accomplice just for opening up your door and letting him crash at your spot for a while.

Always keep in mind that if a jury says that you have helped somebody who committed a crime, no matter how little it was, and whether it was before, during or after the commission of the crime, you can be thrown in the fire as an accomplice for that crime. This means you need to stay away from folks who commit crimes regularly, have plans to commit a crime, or that you think may have committed a crime. If the law finds that you are associated with them in the wrong way it could be hazardous to your freedom.

TO RECAP

- You can be charged with the crime of solicitation if you ask or tell somebody to help you commit a crime.
- You can be charged with the crime of attempt if you try to commit a crime, and that includes something as simple as planning the crime.
- You can be charged with the crime of conspiracy if you agreed to help somebody commit a crime.
- If you engage in a criminal conspiracy, you can be held responsible for every crime that anybody involved in the conspiracy does to help complete the conspiracy, including murder.
- You can be charged with a crime as an accomplice if you help somebody who commits a crime, whether you help them before, during or after the crime.

CHAPTER 4:

OTHER CRIMINAL ACTIVITY TO BE MINDFUL OF

So far, we've talked about some of the major crimes that you can be hit with. Obviously you definitely want to be aware of major stuff that can put you behind bars. At the same time, you should be aware of some minor things that could get you in trouble. A lot of the stuff that we're going to talk about might seem like petty crap that the cops shouldn't even be concerned with. That might be true. But, you still need to avoid doing this stuff. Even though you probably won't get in major trouble for getting caught once; if you get caught again, the system will think that you're a no-good habitual criminal. If the system thinks you're a habitual criminal, it will treat you like trash and try to punish you severely.

Throwing Empty Glass Bottles into Streets and Alleys

Don't throw those empty glass bottles into streets and alleys. As kids, we used to do this one ourselves. We liked to hear the sound of the glass shattering. We were bored, so we did this for entertainment. Little did we know that as bored as we were, we could have ended up even more bored locked in juvenile detention for the summer on some stupid charge like reckless endangerment, destruction of property or disorderly conduct. Throwing glass bottles is a reckless activity, period. Nothing good will ever come from it. But, add the possibility of hitting oncoming traffic and causing an accident, or the impact of one of your bottles injuring or killing somebody, and you possibly have a serious criminal charge on your head.

Setting Stuff on Fire

Quit setting stuff on fire just to see how different things burn. That will burn you one way for sure; you'll end up in a box behind bars. See most people who start fires think the flames are cool, and they are so sure that they can control them. But, setting things on fire really ain't cool at all. And, when you go too far and burn down a house or a building, even if it's vacant and rundown, you run the risk of catching an arson charge. Burning stuff down is foul because people work hard and pay good money to build things. Not to mention that it ain't safe. Arson is serious business and people who get convicted for arson almost always get locked up.

Getting into Fistfights in Public

The streets can be rough, and sometimes you gotta knuckle up. But, you should try hard to avoid getting into physical beef with people because you might get slapped with an assault and/or battery charge. At the very least, you might end up spending a night or two in jail for disorderly conduct.

Threatening People

Besides the fact that threatening somebody can lead to violence, it can also lead to a disorderly conduct charge. And, depending on how you threaten them, it could lead to an assault charge or a charge of terroristic threats, a felony. Keep your mouth closed and your threats to yourself.

Playing your Music too Loud

Yeah, we know you got a boomin' system, but not everybody in the neighborhood wants to hear your music. Why chance the cops runnin' up and shuttin' you down? Just turn the dang music down. You can get a noise violation or disorderly conduct charge for this.

Graffiti and Trashing Public or Private Property

You can do pretty much whatever you want to your own property, but leave other people's stuff alone. Painting and/or trashing public property or private property that doesn't belong to you ain't right. It's also illegal and could net you a criminal charge. In some cases, you can be charged with a felony depending on how expensive it is to fix the damage you cause. The cops won't care that you weren't trying to hurt anybody, and the prosecutor will use you to show how tough on crime she is. The judge will have seen this type of stuff come before his court one too many times, and he will throw the book at you to make an example out of you in the hope that he won't have to deal with more stupid fools like yourself doing this type of silly act.

Underage Drinking

Do we really need to talk about this? If you're under drinking age, wait until you're twenty-one years old before you start hittin' the bottle. You got plenty of time after that to destroy your liver and brain cells to your heart's content. More importantly, you'll stay out of trouble with the cops and your parents.

Being Difficult with the Cops

Whenever the cops are around, always be nice, use a calm voice when talking near them, and do your best to stay out of their way. We tell you this because there is a crime that is very easy to commit, and the cops can arrest you for it if you do the smallest thing. This crime is called "obstruction of justice." Whenever you get in the way of the cops trying to do their jobs, you can be charged with obstruction of justice. When the cops are asking questions in the neighborhood about a crime that happened and you start yelling about how they need to stop harassing innocent people, you can be charged with obstruction of justice. If an officer is trying to investigate an area and you stand in his way, you can be charged with obstruction of justice. So, behave when cops are around.

TO RECAP

- **You can be charged with a crime for throwing empty glass bottles into streets and alleys.**
- **You can be charged with a crime for setting stuff on fire.**
- **You can be charged with a crime for getting in fistfights.**
- **You can be charged with a crime for threatening somebody.**

- You can be charged with a crime for playing your music too loud.
- You can be charged with a crime for making graffiti and trashing other people's property.
- You can be charged with a crime for underage drinking.
- You can be charged with a crime for giving the police a hard time while they are working.

CHAPTER 5:

DEFENSES TO CRIMES—YOUR STORY

Section A: There are Good Reasons Why You Shouldn't Lock Me Up! I'll Show You

The previous pages of this book have outlined some different ways that you can commit a crime. Some on purpose, some carelessly, some accidentally and some just for living like a human being with typical adolescent experiences (see the previous discussion on statutory rape). And, even though we have tried to paint a clear picture for you to see that you're pretty much in danger for half the stuff you do on a weekly, if not daily basis, you are still probably going to continue to do the silly stuff we warned against. So, we are now going to talk to you about defenses, and later we will tell you about the traps of the "justice" system, your rights, and how best to handle yourself when you do find yourself smack dab in the clutches of it.

Most people don't know it, but the wheels of justice start turning against you exactly at the point you decide to do whatever it is that is ultimately going to land you in trouble with the police. It's a pain in the butt, but you really should start living your life today as if you could be in front of a judge and jury tomorrow.

With that said, let's talk about defenses generally. Defenses are basically the excuses or reasons you are going to give the judge and jury for why you are sitting in front of them in a courtroom hoping they don't lock you up. The show is already on the road, you've been booked and charged, and trial is about to be on! Here are your options as defenses:

- You didn't have your facts right,
- You were confused about what the law was. Be careful with this because it doesn't work much and not knowing about a law is not a defense,
- The prosecution failed to prove an element of the crime you're charged with committing beyond a reasonable doubt,
- You were justified in doing what you did, so it wasn't a crime, and
- You were forced against your will to do what you did.

Section B: Basic Defenses Explained

I Didn't Know the Facts

This one is basic. If you thought you were doing something harmless because you had your facts wrong, you shouldn't be charged with a crime. For example, if Zeb was legally firing his assault rifle at a couple of deer for an extreme hunting challenge on a popular hunting ground, but it turns out that he cut down Gus, the dum-dum who refuses to wear the standard hunter's bright orange jump suit, Zeb wouldn't be charged with murder even though he intentionally fired the gun in Gus' direction. Zeb would walk because he thought he was firing at a deer, not Gus, and he didn't mean to kill another human being. This is a pretty fair rule. Zeb shouldn't be charged with a homicide crime if he never meant to kill anybody and really wasn't acting carelessly or recklessly.

But, what if Zeb planned on shooting Gus all along, thinking he could get away with it because he knows Gus never wears his bright colors, but Zeb instead shoots Roscoe Earl by accident? Zeb can't claim he shouldn't be convicted because he was trying to kill Gus, not Roscoe Earl. Zeb's facts were definitely wrong here; he killed the wrong person. Still, Zeb can't claim that he shouldn't be convicted because his facts were wrong. The law says that if your ultimate goal was to commit a crime, it won't matter if your facts were wrong. Zeb's ultimate goal was murder. It doesn't matter that he murdered the wrong person because his facts were wrong. Murder is murder.

I Was Confused About What the Law Was

The basic rule about knowing the law is that the government assumes EVERY INDIVIDUAL IN THE COUNTRY KNOWS ALL OF THE LAWS ON THE BOOKS IN THE COUNTRY. You can never run into the courthouse and say something like, "Hey, I didn't know driving with my cell phone up to my ear was a violation in Chicago, Illinois. I'm from Alaska, you should let me off!" Ignorance of the law is no defense! However, if you get confused about what the law is in a few situations, you can tell the court and they just might give you a break.

One situation where you can claim you didn't know the correct law and ask for a break is when you actually tried to find the correct law and looked in a legitimate place for it, but what you found was incorrect. For instance, if you read a courthouse document that's supposed to tell you the law or listened to a statement made by a law enforcement agent or someone who makes laws, but the law was explained wrong—and you do something illegal based on that bad info, you can use that as a defense. That's because it was the government's fault, they gave you the wrong info.

However, you can't use it as a defense if it turns out you were just being a little slow the day you read or heard it and didn't read or hear it right. If you got the wrong impression about the law because of your own messed up interpretation, you're screwed and your defense won't hold. Also, even if your interpretation is right, but common sense tells you that what you read or heard is probably not true, you won't be able to use that incorrect understanding of the law as a defense then, either. For example, if you found a law that says you are allowed to kill one person once every twenty years and no criminal charges will be brought against you, common sense should tell you that's some crap.

Also, bad advice from a lawyer isn't an excuse either. Make sure you get a good lawyer.

The Prosecution Didn't Prove Every Element of the Crime

This is the basic way to defend yourself against criminal charges. The general rule is supposed to be that you are innocent until proven guilty. For criminal cases, the prosecution is supposed to prove every element of a crime beyond a reasonable doubt for you to be convicted. For something to be proven beyond a reasonable doubt, the prosecutor has to make a case that no reasonable, everyday person could question. If reasonable, everyday people could sit around the dinner table and doubt the crime was committed by you in the way the prosecutor says it was, the prosecutor has not proven her case. For instance, the crime of larceny is broken into five elements: 1) the wrongful taking,(2) and carrying away 3) of the personal property 4) of another 5) with the intent to permanently keep it from them. The prosecutor has to prove that you did all five elements beyond a reasonable doubt, or you walk.

Even if the prosecution can prove beyond a reasonable doubt that you wrongfully took a watch that certainly belonged to another kid (the first 4 elements), but can't prove beyond a reasonable doubt that you intended to keep it from the kid permanently (the fifth element), she can't convict you of larceny. You defend yourself by showing the judge and jury that the prosecution didn't prove you did every element of the crime beyond a reasonable doubt.

I Was Forced Against My Will to Commit a Crime

If somebody threatened to kill or harm you unless you committed a crime for them, you can use that as a defense against criminal charges. You can commit almost any crime involving property, like larceny or burglary if you are forced because somebody threatens to hurt you badly or to kill you if you don't. But, don't get it twisted. You cannot commit murder for somebody else even if they threaten to hurt or kill you if you don't.

I Was Justified in What I Did, so it Wasn't a Crime

Here's where all the fun defenses come in. You can flat out do something that meets the basic elements of a crime, but still avoid conviction if you can put forth an "extremely good reason" for doing what you did. Although the justice system has many flaws, it still tries to be somewhat forgiving by thinking about situations where you just have to straight wild out for justice to prevail. If you have a super good reason for doing what you did, it won't be a crime. We'll explain these "super good reason" defenses in more detail in the next section.

TO RECAP

- Legal defenses allow you to avoid legal punishment even though you would normally be in trouble.
- If you were legitimately confused about whether something is legal or illegal, you may be able to avoid conviction.
- If the prosecution doesn't prove you did every element of a crime beyond a reasonable doubt, you walk.
- You can keep from being convicted if you are justified in your actions, even if they appear to be criminal.

Section C: Self-Defense, Defending Your People & Defending Your Property

Self-Defense

This section will discuss some of those situations when you are justified in doing things that the law really would prefer you didn't do, but understands that sometimes you gotta do what you gotta do. To get it poppin' off with a bang, let's go with every hillbilly homeowner and thuglife gangster's favorite defense, "SELF-DEFENSE!" Gotta get them before they get you, right?

The general rule is that you can use force against somebody else if you believe it's the only way to protect yourself against that person's use of unlawful force against you at that moment. For example, if Malcolm saw Jon-Jon about to run up on him with some violent physical beef, and Malcolm stole on him first and knocked him out, he would be justified, and no charges of assault or battery should stick to him.

Self-defense is indeed a sweet thang because it allows you the freedom to keep yourself from harm without fear of facing punishment by the law. However, claiming self-defense isn't the free-for-all that people think, and we're going to tell you the dangers of acting in what you think is self-defense—and how you may actually be committing a crime when you think you are justified.

First things first, for you to even begin to have a legitimate self-defense argument, you have to reasonably believe that the force that you intend to protect yourself from is unlawful force. That means if the average person wouldn't have thought that the force you were facing was unlawful, your defense doesn't have a chance. An example of unlawful force is when somebody comes up to you and tries to whup upon you for no reason.

Second, if you attack somebody when you don't really believe that it is necessary to protect yourself, and then try to claim self-defense, you are playing yourself. You actually have to believe that force is necessary to protect yourself against the other person's unlawful use of force against you; otherwise, you'll be straight committing a battery, or even murder if you use deadly force. And, don't be trying to fool the judge and jury thinking they'll fall for your game, because the rule in most places is set up so that if the average person in your position would not have thought they needed to bumrush the other person in order to protect himself, your defense won't work. Your fear of danger must make sense. If it doesn't, you can't claim self-defense.

Third, you have to be careful with the amount of force you use to defend yourself. You can't just draw a gun and blaze somebody who was only about to knuckle you up. We know it sucks. You just may have to get your butt whupped in a fist fight like back in the day when everybody wasn't so scared of fightin' with their hands. But, trust, you're better off with a black eye and a few bruises than a murder conviction.

You can only use as much force as necessary to stop the threat of harm to you. If you go beyond that point, you are putting yourself in position to be charged with a crime. The law is particularly concerned about people using deadly force to defend themselves when it's really not necessary. For the most part, you can only use deadly force when you are trying to protect yourself against death, serious bodily injury, forcible rape, or kidnapping. If you don't find yourself in any of these four situations, you better not use deadly force.

Also, in some states, if you could avoid death, serious bodily injury, forcible rape, or kidnapping by walking away or running from the situation, you can't use deadly force. The law would prefer you ran away so no one ends up dead or badly hurt, noteven the asshole threatening you. However, if you are at your house, you don't have to run away, and if you are at work, and a co-worker is threatening you like that, you don't have to retreat. And, you don't have to run away if you are only going to be using non-deadly force.

Fourth, you can't use deadly force to resist an arrest by somebody you know is a law enforcement officer, even if the arrest is unlawful! That means if a dirty cop comes into your house without a warrant, no probable cause or anything, and decides to arrest you, you can't grab your gun and start blasting to keep him from doing it. If you use deadly force to defend yourself in a situation like this you will end up behind bars for a long time, and that's if you are lucky enough to stay alive. What do you really think a dirty cop making an unlawful arrest is gonna do to you once you try to fight back? Technically, you are allowed to use non-deadly force to resist an unlawful arrest, but we tell you this information solely for knowledge's sake, and STRONGLY RECOMMEND AGAINST RESISTING AN ARREST! Chances are, the type of cop that will make an unlawful arrest is the type of cop that would probably beat you to death to keep you from telling your side of the story to a judge and jury. Don't get it twisted. WE REPEAT, WE STRONGLY RECOMMEND AGAINST RESISTING ARREST!

The only situation where you really want to consider raising up on a cop is when the cop is using excessive force to make the arrest. But, keep in mind, the courts didn't find the cops used excessive force against Amadou Diallo, despite shooting 41 shots at him and hitting him 19 times; and he was unarmed. There's not much a cop can do that would be considered excessive force, and the chances of you surviving an altercation with a cop are low no matter what the situation. That's not to say that you shouldn't defend yourself if you feel you are in danger of physical harm from an officer making an unlawful arrest. We're just saying the choice may be between death or prison. You decide.

Fifth, you can't be too wild with your self-defense. If you mess around and hurt an innocent bystander while trying to defend yourself against a threatening wrongdoer, you may be able to claim self-defense for the damage you cause to the wrongdoer, but not for the harm you cause the innocent bystander if the court finds you were straight wildin' and being reckless. Don't think you can fire your gun like crazy in the direction of somebody firing at you from across the street, hit an innocent bystander across the street, and then claim self-defense. Say it with us now, "Jail time!"

Defending Others
The general rule is that you can use force to protect somebody else from unlawful use of force by a threatening wrongdoer. But, just like with self-defense, you can only use the same amount of force being used against the person you're defending. In other words, the amount and type of force you are allowed to use can only go as far as the amount and type of force that the person you are defending could use if he defended himself. Just like with self-defense, there are some ways that you could screw yourself up trying to defend somebody else.

Some states only allow you to claim defense of others if the other person would actually be justified in using force in the situation. If you jump in to help somebody because it appears that the person is having unlawful force used against them, you better be right! If you are wrong, you won't be able to claim the defense. The reason why the law has this rule is to keep people like Malcolm from coming up on a fight

73

between Rob and Jon-Jon, and helping Rob fight off Jon-Jon because he thinks Rob is being wrongfully attacked, all to find out that Rob actually started it. In this situation, Malcolm is actually helping Rob. If you find yourself wanting to be a good Samaritan by protecting somebody from unlawful force, be sure you know what's going on. You could pay a huge price for trying to help somebody.

Defending your Personal Property

You probably wonder exactly what you can do to keep somebody from making you run your property. Can you scream on 'em, smack 'em, kill 'em? How far can you go? The rule is that you can use non-deadly force to prevent somebody from taking your stuff. But, just like with self-defense and defense of others, there are some limits on what you can do to defend your property, so there are some things you must keep in mind when keeping somebody from taking your stuff.

First, remember the rule is that you can only use force to keep another person from taking your stuff. Once they've taken it and had it for a while, you can't use any kind of force at all to get it back. Even though your gym shoes were stolen from your locker during gym last week, and you see the fool who took them wearing them straight up in your face this week like you're his girlfriend or something, you can't run up on him and snatch them back from him without risking criminal assault and/or battery charges. If you didn't try to get them back immediately while he was trying to steal them from you, you're supposed to go tell some authority figure and hope that gets your shoes back. Or you could ask him to give them back. But, straight up, you are probably just screwed in the game for your kicks at that point.

Second, you can only use as much force as necessary to prevent the person from wrongfully taking your stuff. This is a general theme at this point, so by now you should understand that you can't just go off as much as you want just because somebody has done something wrong to you. Some states even require you to first ask the person not to take your stuff. But, if asking them not to take your stuff would increase the chance of some violence going down on you, you don't have to ask. You might have to sneak punch a fool to keep him from taking your stuff.

Third, you can never ever, use deadly force to stop somebody from taking your stuff! It doesn't matter if it's a $30,000 diamond pendant that you just copped to wear at the MTV VMAs. It could even be that brand new $50,000 watch on your arm. You cannot kill somebody to keep them from snatchin' that piece and running off with it. This is the rule surrounding the defense of your property that is most likely to get you into some heat. For example, if you have a gun legally in your possession, and somebody is wrongfully trying to take something from you, it's gonna be hard as hell not to fire off on them instead of trying to wrestle with them. But, you better not pull that trigger. Some states will allow you to pull that thang out and wave it so the person trying to take your property knows they should rethink it. Those states say you can threaten deadly force all you want, you just can't use it. But, make sure you're in one of those states before you go Tony Montana, screamin' and wavin' your gun at everybody coming to get you.

Defending Your Land and Home

We are finally at the point in the discussion where we talk about defending your house. You probably think you can kill anybody who unlawfully attempts to invade your house. For the most part, you're right.

There are a bunch of different rules that apply to when you can defend your home and how far you can go to do it. Some of them say you can't just kill intruders that unlawfully invade your home unless they force themselves in and pose an immediate threat of serious bodily harm to the people inside. However, the way it usually plays out is that you are going to be justified in killing somebody who wrongfully tries to invade your crib. This is because whenever somebody attempts to wrongfully invade the place where you live, it automatically looks like they pose a threat of serious bodily harm to the people inside. But, because there are different rules on the books, there are a few things that you absolutely have to avoid when killing a home invader to tighten up your defense against criminal charges.

First, never kill an invader when he is clearly retreating from the house and no longer presents a threat to anybody inside. If the police show up and the intruder has a bullet hole entering from his back as he's laid out facing outward through the window he came in, it will probably look like you got trigger happy and blasted the dude even though he was no longer a threat to you. In a situation as clear as that, you may see the inside of a cell by the end of the story.

Second, avoid overkill. If you are forced to kill a home invader, do what you gotta do and be done with it. If it takes three shots, or ten jabs with the butcher knife, by all means do that. But, if it only takes three shots or ten jabs, don't shoot nine shots and jab twenty-one times. It starts to look like cold-blooded murder when you get outrageous with it like that, and whenever there's a dead body, you want to avoid looking vicious and overly violent.

TO RECAP
- **You can use force to protect yourself from unlawful force.**
- **You can use force to protect others from unlawful force.**
- **You can only use deadly force when up against deadly force or threat**

of serious bodily harm.

- You can never use deadly force to resist an arrest by somebody you know is a law enforcement officer.
- You can use force to keep somebody from taking your stuff.
- You can only use as much force as necessary to keep somebody from taking your stuff and you can never use deadly force to keep somebody from taking your stuff.
- You can never use any force to take back stuff that somebody took from you and held for a while, even if they took it wrongfully.
- You can use deadly force to protect yourself and everyone in your home, but you cannot use deadly force in your home if no one inside is in danger.

CHAPTER 6:

KEEPING YOURSELF OUT OF TROUBLE WITH THE LAW

Now that you know something about crimes and defenses, let's talk about some of the things you can do to avoid being caught up in criminal activity altogether.

First, if you know that something is illegal, decide in your mind not to do it. If you are somebody who intends to commit crimes, that's your prerogative. But, this book is not going to help you unless you first decide not to be a freakin' criminal. Okay, now that that's out of the way, let's move on.

The next thing you can do is avoid doing stuff that you know will result in a crime or are steps in committing crimes. There aren't many opportunities for you to flirt around with things that are only steps in committing a crime and still avoid being slapped with a charge of criminal activity (see the Sections on Solicitation, Attempt, Conspiracy and Accomplice Liability).

Next, be aware of what you are doing, and all things connected to it. Let's look at the example from earlier where Malcolm got busted for drug trafficking because he thought he could be slick and not ask Rob what was going down. You now know that if you come at the cops and the judge with that lame excuse that you didn't know about no drugs or no money, they are going to slap your tail with a case quick. Basically, you need to ask questions about shady situations that you're about to get involved in.

In the drug trip example, Malcolm would have helped himself a lot if he had asked Rob what was in the bag Rob gave him and what was gonna be in the bag he picked up. If Rob confirmed Malcolm's suspicion that he wanted him to exchange money for his dope, Malcolm could've told him "Hell no," and been on his merry way. That example was simple because it was obvious what was in the bag, but how 'bout we take a different situation where it isn't very clear what's going on. Take this next scenario:

What Malcolm should have done was take a minute to look at the girl, talk to her to see where her head was at, and if she checked out, he should have still thought twice. Now we're not saying you shouldn't have any episodes if they're all to the good, but what we are saying is find out if they really are to the good. Or you could end up in cuffs screaming for your mommy because you thought you and your homie had come up on some freaky stuff.

Most sexual assault laws are only concerned with whether the victim was a willing participant or not. If it turns out that you were screwing around with somebody who didn't want it, it doesn't matter if you didn't know they didn't, if you thought they did want it, or anything like that. All the court is going to do is look at the evidence, see that you had sex, and ask if the victim was willing or not. When she says she didn't want it, you're getting 20-to-life and will have to register as a sex offender...all because you were too excited 'bout the jump-off to ask a few questions.

Also, if you want to keep from catching a case, you have to quit being a reckless knucklehead like you probably tend to be sometimes. Take reckless driving for example. Yeah, yeah, you got skills. You can make that yellow light even though you're a block away from it. And, you can cut that turn right before that oncoming car driving at 50 mph without even thinking about it. Cool, you're sweet behind the wheel, but that's still risky. Not only can it result in your own bodily injury or death, but it can also result in you hurting somebody else and ending up with a case. Seriously injuring yourself may not be at the forefront of your mind since you probably think you're invincible. But, in your twisted thinking, you should at least be concerned about catching a case, so we'll just focus on that for a second.

When you do something like run a traffic light, then hit somebody and get a ticket for it, the government assumes off the top that you were behaving in a criminal manner. The odds may be good that you'll beat the light and won't hit anybody cause you got skills, but if by slim chance something happens to throw you off, like your cell vibrating in your pocket, or some hot chick catching the corner of your eye for a split second, and you miss the light and hit somebody, you're going to be charged like a scrub who can't drive. You might even get a homicide charge if the person you hit dies. That's 20-to-life, just because you are a sweet driver who got caught slippin' for a split second. No need to play yourself like that.

Now, you've learned what laws are, what makes you a criminal, and how you can get caught out there. But, even if you've done the right things and tried to avoid having any run-ins with the cops, you might still get caught up in the legal system. When you're confronted by the cops and the legal system you have certain rights that protect you from getting railroaded. Part II of When the Cops Come Knockin' will explain your rights and talk about some of the tricks the cops use to catch you out there. Read on. It just might save you from prison, or worse.

TO RECAP
- **Decide not to be a criminal. It's the first and biggest step you can take to staying out of prison.**
- **Never flirt with doing things that you know are steps in a crime. It can lead to being a convicted criminal before you know it.**
- **Always ask questions about what you are getting yourself into to make sure you aren't committing a crime.**
- **Calm down the wildin' out and reckless behavior.**

PART II:

THEM RIGHTS YOU ALWAYS HEAR ABOUT

CHAPTER 7:

YOUR CONSTITUTIONAL RIGHTS

High school government was probably boring to you. If you're like most people, you could barely stay awake while your Social Studies teacher droned on and on about the Constitution and Amendments and a whole bunch of other junk that really meant nothing to you. Well guess what? You really, really need to know about your constitutional rights, because knowing about them can save your butt from being thrown in jail. When it comes to dealing with law enforcement, the Constitution and its Amendments give and protect most of your rights.

Constitutional History in Sixty Seconds or Less

We won't bore you with all the historic details. Just like government class, history class bored us too. We'll give you a quick, easy, and painless history lesson on the Constitution and your rights.

During the late 1700s, America was owned by the British empire. The British king was constantly trying to screw the American colonists by taxing them and generally messing with them at his whim. In fact, sometimes the soldiers would just barge in people's houses and go through the colonist's personal papers and stuff. The American folks didn't like being pushed around by the British, so they fought a war against them. The Americans won!

Soon after winning the war, the American leaders decided to form their own country. They sat down and wrote out a paper that set out how the new country was going to be run. They called this paper the Constitution.

The American leaders didn't cover everything they needed to cover when they first wrote the Constitution. In fact, they left out some very important stuff, including rules on preventing the government from messing with people for no good reason as well as rules spelling out rights that each individual American had. They went back to the Constitution and added those rules to it. These rules are called Amendments. The Constitution and Amendments give you your rights. The Fourth, Fifth and Sixth Amendments deal with protecting you from the legal system. You can find the Constitution and the Amendments in any library, Social Studies book or the Internet. Look 'em up sometime. That's the end of the history lesson.

Like we said, quick, easy, and painless. What have you learned so far? That the Constitution protects you from law enforcement abuse by giving you rights that the cops have to respect.

Now here's a basic rule about your rights and the cops: If the cops have to violate your rights to nab you for something, they're breaking the law. If you can point out their violation, you might be able to avoid getting convicted for a crime. This is why you need to know your rights!

Rights Overview

From the time you wake up in the morning to fix breakfast to the time you turn off the light to get cozy with your boo at night, you need to be thinking about 1) keeping the police from illegally searching you and your stuff and 2) not getting arrested.

The good news is that the Constitution says the cops can't just up and do whatever they want to lock you up. You got rights, remember? The Constitution says the cops have to follow rules to arrest you or to search you or your stuff. The bad news is you always have to be on your toes to protect your rights. It's a dirty game out there. Law enforcement can do all kinds of stuff to throw you in jail! The deck is stacked against you, so you gotta keep it tight.

In this section, we're gonna school you on searches and arrests. Pay close attention. It could mean the difference between doing time in the pen like L'il Kim or beatin' the rap like Kels.

CHAPTER 8:

SEARCH & SEIZURE BASICS

Why do the police want to search you and your stuff? Because by searching you and your stuff, they can gather evidence and build a case against you. You can see why it's important to make sure that the cops can't just break into your house and have a look around whenever they want to. There are rules that law enforcement have to follow when they conduct searches. If the cops try to search you or your stuff, those rules kick in and you can do things to keep them in their place.

Section A: Privacy Is The Key

Just because the cops look around you or your property doesn't necessarily mean that they're doing a search. The law's definition of a search is not the same as the dictionary's definition. In order to know what the government considers a search, you have to understand and be familiar with the right to privacy that's given to you by the Constitution. In America you have a right to keep your things private without worrying that some nosy bastard, whether law enforcement or your punk neighbor, can just barge in and see. If the police try to invade your right to privacy, that's a search.

The cops need to get special permission from a judge to search your private things or to invade your privacy. That's the basic rule about privacy and searches. Anything not protected by your right to privacy is fair game. But, here's the problem, what you think is private ain't always what the law says is private. And, in the end, it really doesn't matter what you think.

The law says that two questions have to be asked in order to tell if something is protected by your right to privacy:

1) Did you really expect some level of privacy in the situation?
2) If you did expect some level of privacy, would most other people think that you had a right to privacy in the situation?

The answer to both of these questions has to be yes for you to have privacy protection. Otherwise the law says the cops can go ahead and search you or your stuff without getting permission from a judge.

Some examples of things that you and the law probably agree are private:

*   The inside of your house with the doors closed, and all the window curtains and blinds shut.
*   Your telephone conversations when you are talking dirty on your home telephone with your boo.
*   Your closed purse that holds your emergency tampons in it as you walk down the street.
*   Your pockets holding all that silly change you walk around with annoying everybody, jingling like it's Christmas.

Some examples of things that you may think are private, but the law does not:

*   The inside of your house with the doors and windows wide open. A cop can come stand at your doors and windows and look through them as hard as he likes if they are wide open.

*   Your telephone conversation on your cell phone while you're standing around people who could overhear what you are saying.

*   Your garbage sitting on the side of the curb to be picked up by the garbage man. The police can come scoop up your trash, rip the bag open and ramble through all that stuff to see if you've been up to something.

*   Your fenced-in back yard.

If you ever thought about growing or making drugs or doing any other illegal stuff in your backyard, forget about it. For the most part, you don't really have a right to privacy in your backyard, even if you have a privacy fence. The cops can fly over your property. They can look through fence holes and even climb on top of a nearby building to scope out your yard and find out if you have drugs or other illegal stuff on the property.

The real key to tell if you have a right to privacy is to ask yourself if somebody could easily see whatever it is that you're trying to keep private. Your neighbors could easily look through your open curtains or blinds. Anybody could walk up to your garbage on the curb and tear through it to see what's in it. And, even though not everybody could fly over your back yard in an airplane to see what's back there, as long as planes and helicopters can fly over your property, the cops can use planes and helicopters to spy on it.

TO RECAP
*   **Your right to privacy given to you by the Constitution of the United States protects you from being searched by the police wrongfully.**
*   **If you have an expectation of privacy in a situation, and most other people would have a similar expectation of privacy in the situation, your Constitutional right to privacy kicks in and protects you.**

Section B: Search Warrants and Probable Cause

Search Warrants

Once it looks like the cops are going to try to do a search and invade your privacy, they have to get a search warrant. A search warrant is basically a permission slip signed by a judge. It gives the cops the right to search your stuff.

Police officers gotta hit the judge with some really good reasons to get a search warrant. Once they give the judge their reasons, he issues the search warrant. Instead of using the words "good reasons," the law uses the words "probable cause." Really, the cops must have probable cause to get a search warrant.

Probable Cause

When it comes to searches, probable cause is anything that cops can point to that would make the average cop with his experience as a cop think a crime was committed and that evidence of that crime will be found in the places the cop wants to search. Its gotta be more than just a hunch, though. The cops can't just tell the judge, "Your honor, he just looked like he was up to something, and I was pretty sure I would find evidence of a crime if I searched his stuff." It's gotta be some pretty convincing stuff. For example:

The cops don't give Malcolm an apology. They don't help put his crib back in order. And, they don't pay him money to repair the stuff they broke. And, Malcolm can't sue them, report them or do anything, because technically, their search was all good. It was all good because they had probable cause and a search warrant. See, any average cop with experience fighting crime could think that the gas station was robbed because there was an emergency call claiming a gas station was robbed. And, any average cop with experience would think that Malcolm committed the crime and that evidence of the crime would be found at Malcolm's house based on the description given by the cashier.

Here's something else you should know. It's usually pretty easy for a cop to convince a judge that he has probable cause to get a search warrant. After all, cops and judges usually think of themselves as being on the same team. Guess who's on the opposite team? YOU! Judges, prosecutors and cops see each other every day. They sometimes eat together or have drinks after work. Hell, they may sometimes even watch the Sunday football game at each other's house. In other words, they're gonna work together to screw you!

TO RECAP

- The police must have a search warrant to invade your right to privacy.
- A search warrant is a permission slip given by a judge that says the police can invade your right to privacy.
- The police must have probable cause to get a search warrant.
- Probable cause is anything the average cop with his experience could use to justify his belief that a crime was committed, that a particular person committed the crime and that evidence of that crime could be found in a specific place.

Section C: The Cops Running Your Stuff and Seizures

In the example above where Officers Petti and Grimes searched Malcolm's house for evidence of the gas station robbery, if they had found some cash and a Snickers in a drawer, a shotgun hanging on Malcolm's bedroom wall, and 4 packs of Kools sitting on the kitchen counter, they could have taken all that stuff from Malcolm's house as evidence of the robbery. When the police take your stuff, that's called a "seizure." The Constitution says the police have to play by the rules when they do a seizure just like they have to play by the rules when they do a search. In this example, the police did play by the rules because they had probable cause, showed probable cause to a judge and got a warrant, and took stuff that looked like evidence of the crime they were doing the search for. A quick side note: the "stuff" the police take is sometimes something weird like your blood, or a pee sample, or even a body part, like a toenail or hair. If the cops take something like that from you, that's a seizure too, and they have to follow the rules then too.

On top of having probable cause, the cops have to follow some other rules when it comes to doing searches and seizures. Every search warrant they use has to say what places, people, and things can be searched. Police officers are only allowed to search at the places specifically listed on the search warrant to find the specific people and things listed on the warrant. And, they can only do a search of the people and things specifically listed on the warrant.

But, know this, even though the cops can only search the people listed on the warrant, if the cops reasonably suspect that somebody hanging out at your house might have a weapon on them, they're allowed to pat down that person for weapons. They can pat the person down even if their name isn't listed on the warrant. Here's an example:

Malcolm goes over to Carlos' house to hang out. All of a sudden, a S.W.A.T. team busts in through Carlos' front door and they have a warrant! It's a drug raid, and the cops think Carlos is a drug dealer. Most drug dealers hold heat. To protect themselves from getting shot, the cops are gonna pat Carlos down to make sure he doesn't have a gun. The cops also figure that any dude who hangs around a dealer is probably holding heat too. Yep, you guessed it, they're gonna pat Malcolm down too.

Malcolm's name isn't on the warrant but he still gets patted down by the cops because he's viewed as possibly dangerous. When the cops' safety is at risk, they can pat down anybody who could be dangerous.

TO RECAP
- When the police take your stuff during a search, that's called a seizure. Sometimes the stuff seized can be something weird like your blood, your pee, your spit, or even a body part.
- The police must have probable cause to seize your stuff.
- The police can only search and seize things that are listed on their search warrant.
- To keep themselves safe, the police don't need a search warrant for people who could be dangerous to them while they are doing the search.

Section D: Keepin' Your Stuff Outta Sight Keeps You Outta Jail

We told you that cops can only look for stuff specifically listed on a warrant. Sounds pretty simple, right? But, guess what? The cops can also take any illegal stuff they happen to come across not listed on the warrant if you leave it out in the open. This is called the "plain view rule." Say the cops get a warrant to specifically look for a stolen computer at your house. They show the warrant to you and you let them in. But, uh oh! You suddenly remember that you left your weed stash out on your bedroom dresser. Now you're in big trouble, because they can snatch that stuff up and use it to nail you on a drug charge. The funny thing is they might not even find a computer but you're is still going to jail.

The plain view rule applies to sounds and smells too.

Let's say instead of drugs on top of a dresser, you have a friend smoking weed in one of your rooms. As the cops are looking for the computer, they smell the weed. They also hear your boy say, "Yeah boy, I'm high as hell off this weed."

Well, the smell of the herb, and the voice of your stupid homeboy are both in plain view because they could easily be smelled and heard by the officers. That means your idiot homie and the weed are gonna get snatched up. The cops will usually try to pin the weed on your friend and YOU. What does this mean for you? It means you better be careful about what, and sometimes who, you leave out in the open when the cops come knockin'.

The cops can also take out-in-the-open stuff that ain't illegal if they reasonably believe it would help them make a case against you, regardless of whether it's listed on the warrant or not. That's right, it doesn't have to be anything like drugs or stolen property. It could be stuff like duct tape, or rope, or even something like your MP3 player, as long as they reasonably believe it had something to do with a crime.

TO RECAP

- When the police are conducting a search, they can take anything that they can see, hear, smell or touch if it clearly looks, feels, sounds or smells like criminal evidence.
- When the police are conducting a search, they can take anything that they can see, hear, smell or touch if it looks like something that was used to commit a crime, even if it isn't clearly criminal evidence.

Section E: Hangin Out With The Cops While They Do A Search

If the cops get a warrant to search for stuff at your house, they can force you to stay at the crib while they're looking for it. They're allowed to do this so you don't get ghost if they find something in the house that they can use as evidence against you in court. Plus, having you within sight shrinks the chance of you coming back with a weapon to bust their asses with.

Now that you know all of this stuff, the real question is, how do you protect yourself when the cops come knockin'?

CHAPTER 9:

WHAT TO DO WHEN THE COPS COME KNOCKIN'

Section A: First Contact With The Cops

If the cops come knockin', you got two choices. You can either ignore them or you can answer the door. Of course, if they have an arrest warrant and reasonably think you're hiding inside, they might end up busting through the door anyway. If you decide to answer the door and the cops say they have an arrest warrant, you should go outside to talk to them. Make sure to shut the door behind you when you do. On the other hand, if they don't say they have an arrest warrant, don't step outside. Talk to them from inside the house, preferably with the door slightly open. We'll explain more in Chapter 12 about what to do if the cops come knockin' with an arrest warrant. For now, though, we're just concentrating on what to do when the cops come with a search warrant.

Section B: What To Do If The Police Have A Search Warrant

If the police ask to come in, calmly ask them from behind your closed door if they have a search warrant. If they say, "yes," open the door and read it to make sure that it's legit. Make sure that the warrant has the correct address, that the date on the warrant is fairly recent (usually no more than a couple of weeks) and that it has a judge's signature. When we say that the warrant has to have the correct address we mean that it should have your exact address. If you live in an apartment or condo, it should have your apartment number and not just the building number. If the warrant has the wrong address, is too old, or isn't signed by a judge, it's not legit. An illegit warrant means the cops aren't allowed to come in. But, you have to tell them that you don't consent to them searching your home or your stuff because the warrant is not right. How do you do that? Just say, "Officer, the address on this warrant is wrong (or the date is more than a few weeks old, or this warrant wasn't signed by a judge) so I do not consent to you searching my home or my things."

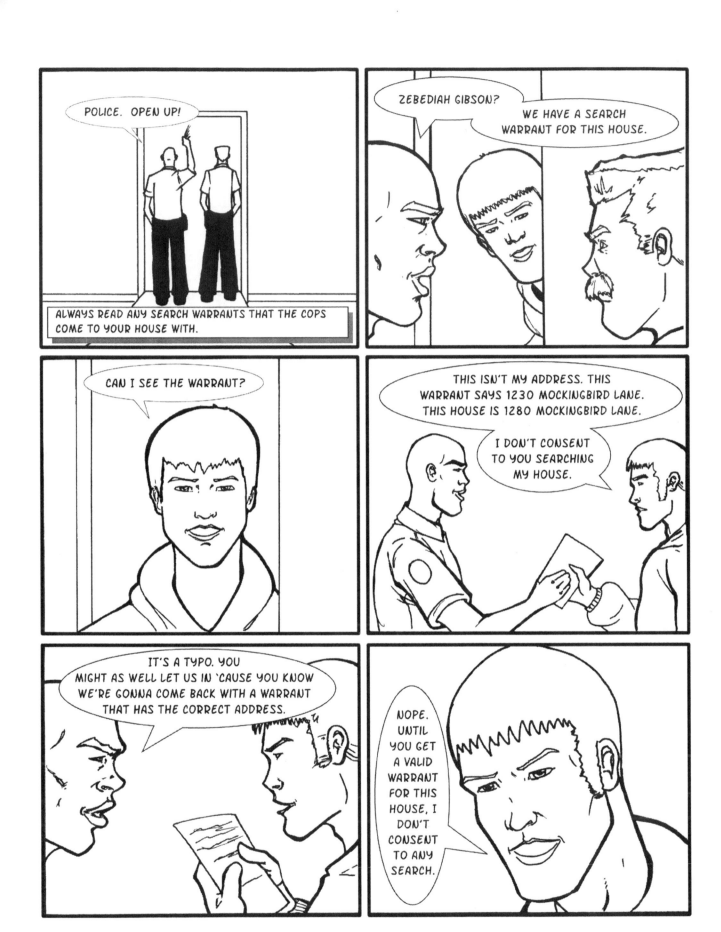

Just in case you're wondering if you should try to physically stop the cops from coming in, the answer should be obvious. Heck no! One of three things will probably happen. The cops will either A) decide not to go in, B) beat your brains out, arrest you and go in anyway or C) shoot and kill you. If you're a male, and especially if you're a minority, scenario B and C are more likely to happen than if you're white or female. Be smart and just let them do their thing. When it's time, make sure you tell your attorney that the cops didn't listen to you when you told them that you weren't giving them permission to search.

When the cops search your stuff, don't expect them to handle your things with love. They may just trash your crib. And, if they do, they ain't gonna clean up the mess either. If this happens, you need to take pictures of your place after the cops have trashed it and give those pictures to your attorney, they might be helpful down the line in your case.

TO RECAP
- Always read any search warrant that a cop shows you very closely.
- If a warrant isn't legit, you can keep the cops from searching your stuff.

Section C: Can We Have Permission, Pretty Please?

The easiest way for a cop to get in and search your house, your stuff or even you without getting a warrant is by getting your permission. The police can search your house and/or your personal things without a warrant if you tell them it's cool. Cops sometimes try to trick people into giving permission to search. For instance, a cop might walk up to you on the street real friendly asking to check out your bag. He'll say something like, "Hey mind if I take a look in your duffle bag?" Or he may reach for your bag and say, "You don't mind do you?" Without thinking you say, "No, I don't mind." Next thing you know, he's going through your bag.

IF A COP **IS** ARRESTING YOU, HE CAN LOOK THROUGH THE STUFF YOU HAVE ON YOU LIKE YOUR BAGS AND EVEN YOUR POCKETS. ON THE OTHER HAND, IF THE COPS DON'T HAVE A LEGAL BASIS FOR BEING ABLE TO GO THROUGH YOUR STUFF, FOR INSTANCE, IF THEY'RE NOT ARRESTING YOU OR THEY DON'T HAVE A WARRANT, THEY CAN'T LOOK INSIDE YOUR BAGS OR POCKETS WITHOUT **YOUR** PERMISSION. USUALLY THE REASON THEY ASK YOUR PERMISSION IS BECAUSE THEY DON'T HAVE ANY LEGAL BASIS. SOMETIMES THEY'LL TRY TO TRICK YOU BY SOUNDING AS THOUGH THEY'RE ORDERING YOU TO OPEN UP YOUR STUFF FOR THEM WHEN THEY'RE REALLY JUST ASKING. ALWAYS ASK THE POLICE IF THEY'RE ASKING OR ORDERING YOU.

A quick note: drug-sniffing dogs are big trouble in these situations. A cop can get probable cause if a drug-sniffing dog smells drugs in your bags. If he stalls you long enough for a drug-sniffing dog to come and the dog starts going crazy because he smells drugs in your bags, the cop then has probable cause to search your bags without your permission and can run all through your stuff. Try to keep it moving once you've told the cops they don't have permission to search your bags. Otherwise, that K9 might get you hemmed up!

If the cops don't have a warrant, but ask to search your house, it is your right to tell them you don't give them permission to search your house. You do this by saying, "Officer, I do not give you permission to search my house or my things." Yes, you'll sound like a square. Do it anyway. When you use slang or street talk, cops pretend they don't understand what you are saying. Anyway, try to keep the conversation short. The longer you talk, the greater the chance you'll mess up and say or do something that will allow the cops to legally search your stuff. Here are some of our most important statements to you. IT IS NEVER A GOOD IDEA TO LET THE COPS INTO YOUR HOUSE WITHOUT A WARRANT! IT IS NEVER A GOOD IDEA TO GIVE THE COPS PERMISSION TO SEARCH YOUR BAGS OR ANY OTHER CONTAINERS WITHOUT A WARRANT. IN OTHER WORDS, ITS NEVER A GOOD IDEA TO CONSENT TO A SEARCH. GOT IT? GOOD!

It doesn't matter how intimidating they try to act. If the cops don't have a warrant, they gotta get your permission to look through your stuff or to go inside your house. The exception is when somebody is in danger or the cops are chasing a suspect and he runs inside the house. In this situation the cops can go into the house. Also, the cops can go inside your house without a warrant and without permission when they think someone inside will get rid of evidence (like flushing dope down the toilet).

Permission to Search Has to be Voluntary

In order to give the cops permission to search your house properly, your permission always has to be voluntary. The cops are never supposed to force you to let them do a search. Your permission isn't voluntary if the cops trick you into letting them in by lying about having a warrant. Your permission isn't voluntary if they flex on you by showing their weapons. It isn't voluntary if they nag and nag you for your permission after you've told them no over and over. It isn't voluntary if they take advantage of the fact that you are young, a minor, or mentally disabled. Finally, it isn't voluntary if they try to make you think that they are just going to do whatever they want no matter what you say by grouping up and scowling and yelling at you. Again, the best thing to do if the cops ask to search your house or your stuff is to say, "Officer, I do not consent to you searching my house or my things." Always tell your lawyer if the cops pressured you to give them your consent to search.

You Wanna Play Mr. Nice Guy with the Cops

If for some reason you decide to give the cops permission to search your house, tell them exactly where they can search. When we say "exactly" we mean "exactly." You better be real precise and tell them that they can only look in certain rooms or areas. The cops aren't supposed to go into rooms that you don't give them permission to go into. But, if you don't tell them exactly where they can search, they are entitled to look any and everywhere. Also, remember the plain view rule. If anything incriminating is left out in the open, it's over for you.

You can even tell the cops to stop at any point. If possible, you should have somebody with you to witness the instructions that you give the cops, just in case the cops decide to ignore you and you end up in court. But, really, even though we hate to sound like a broken record, the best thing to do if the cops want to search your house or your stuff is to demand that they get a warrant.

Your Roommates, Live-ins, and Exes Can Screw You in the Game

When you are trying to avoid giving the police permission to search your home, you have to be extra careful if you have a roommate or a live-in boyfriend, or girlfriend, or even an ex who still has a key. These people can screw you big time by giving the cops permission to come into your house or apartment even if you haven't. The law says they can.

Your roommate can give the police permission to search any areas that you share like your living room, kitchen or general basement area. On the other hand, your roommate can't give the cops permission to go into any area that you don't both share, like your private bedroom, closets or a basement that you don't allow them to use. Those places are off limits. The only catch is that you have to make extra sure you let your roommate know that he or she ain't allowed to be in those areas you want protected. If you don't make it clear, the law says that your roomie can give permission for the cops to enter any area you both have access to, including your room.

Live-ins can also give the cops permission to search your house. Here's an example:

*Drug making activities are wrong and illegal. The authors use this example only to illustrate search and seizure laws.

When Zeb returns home, he's gonna want to pimp slap Bunny because she just sent him to jail for at least twenty years. He should have listened to his boys and never moved her into the house in the first place. You know how you were thinking about asking for the key to your apartment back from your trifling ex-girlfriend? Well now you've got a good reason to take that stuff back. If you let her keep it and she lets the cops into your house while letting them believe she is still living there, you might need to tell all your friends you'll be seeing them in 5 to 10. In other words, she can let the cops in even though she doesn't live there anymore, so long as she does not tell the cops she doesn't live there anymore. Get it straight right now playa, as long as she has a key and the cops believe that she lives there, she can burn you. And, they always believe she lives there. Play it safe and get your key back. You know you should anyway.

And, don't sleep on the power of your kids. They can let the cops in to do a search too. Be sure to tell your kids to never give the cops permission to come into your house without a warrant unless the house is on fire or somebody is in danger inside the house. Teach your kids how to read and talk to them about warrants. In the hood, too many kids can't read as well as they should and may get tricked by a cop waving around some paper saying that it's a warrant when it really isn't. Actually, they use this trick on illiterate adults too. If you don't know what the word "illiterate" means, you're a prime target. Look it up!

If you know there will be times that you won't be home with your kids, tell the oldest or whichever kid is the smartest to ask the cops — from behind a closed door — if they have a warrant when the cops come knockin'! Tell your kid to ask to see the warrant if the cops say yes. Then tell him to go outside to read the warrant and to be sure to shut the door behind him. Then pray that you taught your kids well. Make sure that they know that the address has to be correct, that the date should be fairly recent and that a judge is supposed to sign. Yeah, we know this seems like a lot to put on your kids, but just like you, kids have to be smart when it comes to dealing with the cops. Even if your kid is a little knucklehead D- student, you better make sure he's an A+ student of this small law lesson. Now if this isn't a good enough reason to help your kids with their reading, what is?

TO RECAP

- If you give the cops permission, they don't need probable cause or a search warrant to do a search.
- Never give the cops permission to do a search.
- For you to properly give the cops permission to search your stuff, it has to be voluntary; otherwise it isn't legit permission and their search will be illegal.
- Anyone living in your house and anyone with open access to your house can give the police permission to search your house, so give strict instructions to all of your roommates to never let the police search it.
- Get your keys back from your ex!
- Teach your kids how to read!

Section D: If It's Your Party, It's Your Butt On The Line

Who doesn't like a good party? Every once in a while, we all cut loose at a good party and relax. That's cool. But, if you're the party thrower, you'd better make sure that you maintain control over the situation. Make sure you make it clear to your party people that they cannot bring weapons, drugs or any other illegal things into your party whether it be at your crib or a place that you've rented. You know Jon-Jon who's always starting some drama? Leave him off the invite list.

Tell your friends to keep your front and back doors closed and locked during the party. If you don't, the cops can come into the party without a warrant or asking permission just like anybody else who was coming to the party. Also, make sure to check around the house during the party to make sure that your guests are not doing any illegal stuff like smoking weed. Remember, when somethin' goes down at your house, it's your butt that's on the line.

When the cops show up at your party and there is weed smoke in the air and stems and seeds laid out on the counter, they ain't gonna listen when you say, "That stuff ain't mine," or "I ain't even know those fools were upstairs smokin' that weed!" They're gonna be like, "Yeah, tell it to the judge, you weed party-throwin' bastard!" And, even if it isn't yours, if it's laid out or being passed around the party for anybody who wants it, you have access to it just like the person who brought it, so you could end up on the hook that way as well.

TO RECAP
- When you throw a party, you can be held responsible for anything brought in and out of the party spot, including drugs, weapons and other illegal items.
- If the doors to your party are freely open, the cops can come in and look around as they see fit, so keep your doors closed and secured.

CHAPTER 10:

RIDIN' AND ROLLIN' IN THE DANGER ZONE

Section A: Your Car Ain't Safe

Remember that right to privacy we talked about earlier? Well you don't have much of it when it comes to your car. Your car has clear glass windows in the front, the back and around all sides. Anyone can see right through it. In fact, when you take it on the streets, a bunch of people probably look inside it every day. The law says that because it's easy to see through your car and since people see inside it all the time, you don't have a real expectation of privacy inside it.

Also, cars get up and go. Because a car that might have evidence of a crime in it can be in one place one minute and moved to another place and cleaned out in the next minute, cops are allowed to get after it without jumpin' through all the hoops they would normally have to jump through if they want to search your house.

Since you don't have much of a right to privacy inside your car and your car can roll out at any time, if cops stop you out somewhere and have probable cause to believe that your car has evidence of a crime or illegal stuff in it, they don't need a search warrant to look through it. But, they do have to be able to explain in clear words what they are suspicious of when they try to search your ride without a warrant. Whenever you get stopped and a cop attempts to search your car, you should ask them why. If they can't explain it to you clearly, then you may refuse to be searched. After refusing the search, ask if you are free to leave. At that point, if the officer cannot explain clearly why he would like to search your car, he is supposed to let you go.

If the cops stop you and can explain clear reasons for wanting to search your car, they can take you down to the station, and take your car to an impound so they can search it there without a warrant. They can also impound your car, hold it for a few days, and then search it later without a warrant. The only bit of protection you have is if they come pick you up from your house. If the cops come get you from your house, they can't search your car without getting a warrant first, and they definitely can't take your car away from the house without getting a warrant first. The cops are not allowed to open your locked trunk without a warrant; and they can't open a locked glove box without a warrant either.

TO RECAP

- If the cops have probable cause to believe there is evidence of a crime in your car, they don't need to go get a search warrant to run through it.
- If the cops stop you on the road and arrest you, and they have probable cause to believe there is evidence of a crime in your car, they can take your car to impound and search it there even after holding it for a few days.
- If the cops arrest you at home, they cannot take your car down to the station without a warrant to search your car also.

Section B: The Bags & Containers In Your Car Ain't Safe Either

Whenever the cops can legally search your car, with or without a warrant, they can also search any container found in the car without going to get a warrant. By container we mean anything that can hold something. A container might be a box, a suitcase, a paper bag or even something like a bottle. It could also be something like a gun case. And, it doesn't matter whether the container is open or closed.

More specifically, the cops can search a container found in your car without a warrant in two different situations. The first situation is when the cops have probable cause to search a car without a warrant, and they find a container inside the car. They can open that container without getting a warrant and search it too. But, they can only search the container in this situation if it is actually large enough to hold the criminal stuff that they have probable cause to look for. For instance, they couldn't open up your girlfriend's purse hoping to find a shotgun. The second situation is when the cops have probable cause to think they will find a particular container holding criminal evidence inside your car. In this situation they can search your car for the container, and then search inside the container once they find it.

The police can even take a container out of your car and hold it for a few days at the police station before searching it. They would probably be pushing it if they kept it for some months and then searched it without a warrant, but they can hold your stuff for a minute though. They can also take a container that belongs to somebody riding with you, even if they aren't suspected of committing any crimes.

TO RECAP

- The police can search inside bags and other containers that are inside your car, without having a warrant, if they have probable cause to search your car.
- The cops can search inside your car for a bag or container, without having a warrant, if they have probable cause to believe a bag or container containing evidence of a crime is inside your car.
- The cops can take and search a container belonging to anyone riding in the car with you, without having a warrant, if they have probable cause to believe there is evidence of a crime in that container.

Section C: What To Do When You Get Pulled Over

If you get pulled over by the cops, act natural, stay relaxed and wait for the officer to approach the car. NEVER GET OUT OF YOUR CAR UNLESS THE OFFICER TELLS YOU TO...unless you feel like dying or getting a beat down. Keep your hands in plain sight, comfortably on the steering wheel for the cop to see. Avoid grabbing the steering wheel tight because it makes cops nervous. Roll down your window and speak pleasantly to the officer. Look directly at him when you speak. Always have your registration and insurance in a place where you don't have to fumble around to get it. If your papers are in your glove box, calmly tell the officer that they are in there and ask if it is okay for you to reach inside to get them. Get your registration out of the glove box only after the officer says it's okay to do so, and do it calmly. If the cops think you're reachin' for some heat, you just might get blazed before you turn around with your papers.

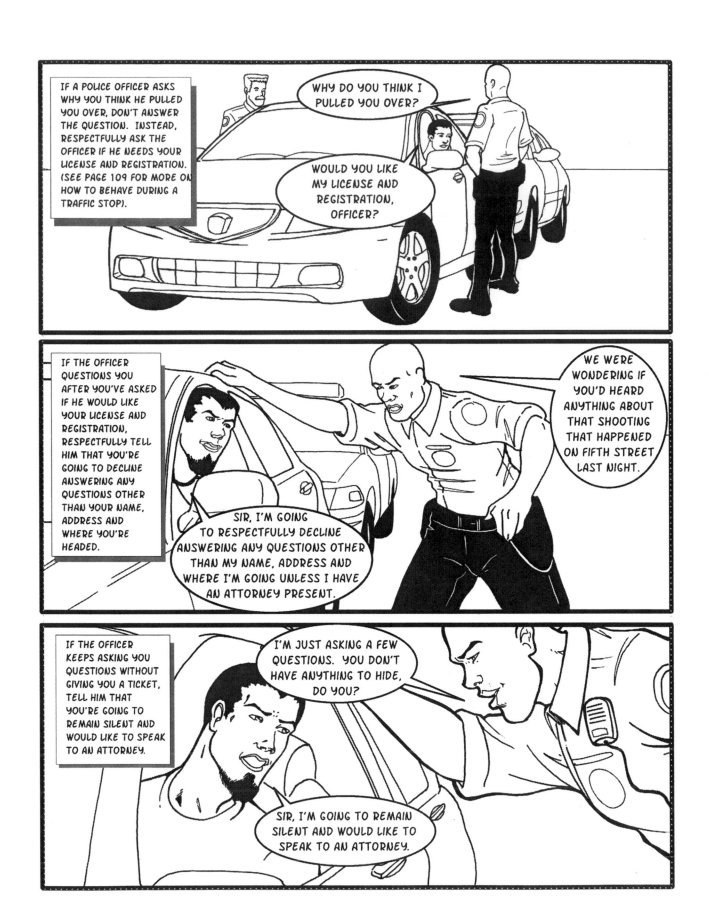

When the cops ask you questions about who you are, what you're doing and where you're going, answer briefly and don't volunteer any extra info. Talking details is a no-no. The more you talk, the bigger hole you dig and the more crap you give the cops to get you with. Keep it simple. And, make sure that all of your partners in the car do the same. Above all, be polite and respectful to the cops and don't go yelling at them about what they can and can't do to you, how you know your rights or any other thing like that. Shootin' off your mouth might get your mouth shot off. Hopefully, if you've done the above, they'll let you ride out.

When the cops return your license and registration, ask if you're free to leave. They may ask to search your car. You, of course, tell them that you don't give permission to search your car. Then ask again if you are free to leave. If he says yes, go ahead and ride out. If the cops don't tell you that you are free to leave, request to speak with a lawyer. Then remain silent until you get to speak to your lawyer.

TO RECAP
- Whenever you ride out in you car, always have your license, registration and insurance in a place where you can get to it easily and without fumbling around.
- Whenever you are pulled over by the police, be calm, cool and polite.
- If a cop asks for your permission to search your car, tell him "no!"
- As soon as the officer returns your license, insurance and registration (and/or ticket if they give you one), ask him if you are free to leave. If he says no, ask for a lawyer and be quiet until you get one!

CHAPTER 11:

SPECIAL SEARCH SITUATIONS

Section A: Overview Of Special Searches

We've already talked about the basic search and seizure situations and rules and hopefully you now have a general understanding of how basic searches and seizures should go. But, there are some special search and seizure situations that don't follow the basic rules so you need to know about those as well:

- Administrative searches,
- Border searches,
- Checkpoint searches,
- Public school searches,
- Airport searches,
- Government job searches, and
- Probation and parole searches.

We'll explain each of these searches below.

Section B: Administrative Searches

Government officials like building inspectors (not police officers) can, in some situations, search your property without a warrant if they're conducting an administrative search. An administrative search is a search that the government does to protect the safety and welfare of the general public. For instance, when a building inspector is checking to see that your apartment or other building is up to safety code, he's doing an administrative search. While he's in there checking to see if you have a smoke detector and that your water heater is stored in a safe place, he just might go ahead and search for drugs, guns or other illegal stuff, without your permission to do so and without a warrant. The good news is that a building inspector can't arrest you or take your stuff as evidence. The bad news is that a building inspector can go tell the police what he saw. Once he tells the police, the police can use it as probable cause to get a warrant to conduct a police search. Once they come back and search you with that warrant, you're done.

Although building inspectors can come through and do searches without warrants, they still have their own rules to follow. First, they can never come into your house that you own without your permission. Second, building inspectors are usually not allowed to come in the middle of the night to do an inspection, not even to inspect a building that isn't your home. If an inspector came to your apartment in the middle of the night to do an inspection, and found some illegal stuff and reported it to the police, the police couldn't use it against you.

Still, the main point is this, don't sleep on building inspectors. Building inspectors make great snitches.

Section C: Border Searches

A lot of your rights go out the window at the border. Understand this, at the border, the cops can stop you and ask you questions even if they don't notice anything particularly shady about you. However, they can't search your car without probable cause. But, if they end up noticing something shady about you, they can hold you for a longer time than they could if you weren't at the border. How long can they keep you? Who knows? The cops have been known to keep a person at the border for up to 16 hours. A judge, the cops' favorite buddy, will ultimately decide if the cops kept you too long. You already know what the answer is going to be.

Section D: Fixed Checkpoints

The police can set up special spots on the road and stop all cars that pass those spots to ask drivers and passengers questions. These spots are called checkpoints. The police don't need to suspect anything in particular to stop the cars that pass through these checkpoints. And, as they ask questions, they usually peek inside the cars for anything suspicious. If even the smallest thing catches their attention, they will have probable cause to search your ride.

Section E: Narcotics Checkpoints

If you fall for this one, you probably deserve to be locked up. If you see a sign that says there's a drug or weapons checkpoint ahead, DO NOT TOSS ANYTHING OUT OF YOUR CAR. This is exactly what the cops want you to do. The cops figure that you'll be so afraid of getting caught that you will dump evidence before you get to the checkpoint. And, they'll be hiding, watching and waiting in the bushes ready to nab that stuff. The cops can't set up actual checkpoints to try and catch people with drugs anyway, but they can set up signs that fake you out. Still, don't get it twisted, the cops can set up checkpoints to check and see if people are driving drunk. Read on.

Section F: Sobriety Checkpoints

Cops are allowed to set up checkpoints to see who's driving drunk on the roads. If the cops want to catch you with drugs in your car all they have to do is set up a sobriety checkpoint. They'll stop you at the checkpoint and pretend that they're checking for drunk drivers and then start questioning you about whether you have drugs in the car. But, you don't have to answer any questions about drugs or any other criminal activity at these checkpoints. If the cops start asking you questions about drugs or other criminal activity, you can refuse to answer those questions.

Section G: Airports

The airport is just like the border, you basically have very few rights. Once you go through airport security, the cops can search you without a warrant, without probable cause, and even without noticing anything shady at all. Be smart and don't do things that increase your chances of being hassled. Come to the airport clean, neat, and dressed like the average Midwestern square. Dress like this even if its not normally your style. In other words, break out the khaki pants/shorts and button-up shirt.

Leave the excessive jewelry at home. Walking around the club on a Friday night with a fat knot in your pocket might impress the ladies and might even get you some play, but at the airport the only thing its gonna get you is attention from the police. Paying for plane tickets with cash will set off all kinds of bells for security folks at the airport. What are some other things that trigger airport security? Here are a few examples:

- Showing up at the airport with no luggage,
- Being young, single, and male, and
- Looking nervous or being fidgety.

You don't want airport police to snatch you up. If they ask you to follow them, they're likely taking you to the "small room." The trip to the small room could end up being an embarrassing experience. If the cops think you have a weapon, they will pat you down. If they think you have drugs they will search you inside and out. Don't worry about the cops getting all up in your face, you need to be worried about them getting all up in somewheres else. Bottom line, DO NOT BRING DRUGS TO THE AIRPORT!

Section H: Public Schools

Public school principals and other school administrators don't need a warrant or probable cause to search your locker, your bags or anything else. They only need what's called "reasonable grounds." Reasonable grounds is less than probable cause. Reasonable grounds just means that the school official reasonably thinks he might find somethin' if he does a search.

It doesn't take much to have reasonable grounds. For instance, there could be reasonable grounds for a search of your locker if you always keep your books and jackets in your girlfriend's locker, but you still go to and from your own locker all the time and never seem to put anything in it or take anything out of it. There could be reasonable grounds to search your coat if you are rockin' it even though it's too warm to be wearing that heavy jacket. There could be reasonable grounds to search under your hat if you refuse to take it off like school rules say.

Section I: Government Employees

If you work for the government, your employer can search and snatch up your stuff to find out if you've been screwing up or stealing on the job. They are also allowed to drug test you. They aren't allowed to test you with the purpose of bringing you up on criminal charges, but they can test you to make sure you aren't getting high or drunk because that could make you screw up on the job. For instance, alcoholic bus drivers— not a good thing. They also aren't allowed to test you just because they want to send a message that drugs are "bad."

Section J: People On Probation

Probation is when you've been found guilty of some crime, but the judge decides not to send you to lockup. Instead the judge basically tells you that the law will be watching you for a certain amount of time to make sure that you keep your nose clean. The catch is that if you do some dirt while on probation, the court will drop the hammer, and you will do some time behind bars.

The police do not need a warrant to stop and search you or to come into your house if you're on probation. As a matter of fact, they can get at you for just about any old thing. Why? Because technically, when you're on probation, you are actually serving a sentence, you just get to do it outside of jail as long as you act right. People in jail don't have any right to privacy and can be searched and snatched up whenever the government feels like it. If you are on probation, the same rules pretty much apply and you can be searched and snatched up whenever.

TO RECAP

- Building inspectors don't need a warrant to search your house.
- Border patrol and customs officers don't need a warrant to search your stuff when you cross over international borders.
- Cops are not allowed to set up checkpoints to catch people with drugs.
- Cops are allowed to put up fake narcotic checkpoint signs to trick people into tossing drugs out of their cars.
- Cops are allowed to set up checkpoints to catch drunk drivers.
- Airport officials don't need a search warrant to search your stuff.
- School officials can search your stuff for even the smallest reason.
- Government employers can search and take your stuff to find out if you've been screwing up or stealing stuff.
- The cops can search people who are on probation without a warrant any time and for any reason.

CHAPTER 12:

ARRESTS

Section A: What Is An Arrest?

We just finished talking about the basic rules that the cops have to follow in order to search and seize your stuff. Now we are about to talk about the basic rules they have to follow when it comes to snatching you up and seizing you! That's right, we're talking about arrests. Just like with searches, knowing when you are under arrest is important because you have certain rights that kick in as soon as an arrest begins. If you want to know what's up in case you are arrested, pay close attention to this section.

To understand arrests, first you need to know about being detained by the police and police detention. Whenever the cops take you to any place where they hold you and get at you about a crime, or whenever the cops stop you and ask you questions, they are detaining you and you are under police detention.

Police detention becomes an arrest whenever you are not free to leave when you want. To say it another way, if you are ever taken somewhere by the police, or if the police stop you somewhere, and you are not free to get up and leave whenever you feel like it, you are under arrest even if they haven't said so.

People end up having problems knowing that they are under arrest because it's never easy to tell if you are free to leave police detention. The cops will never stop you and say, "We want to ask you a few questions, but you can leave whenever you like (and you don't have to tell us anything)." And, heck, anybody can stop you in the street and ask you a question, it's a free country. When the cops come up getting all nosy, you might not take it that seriously. But, chances are when the boys in blue are asking you questions on the street, they ain't just shootin' the breeze. Most times they're trying to find out what you know about some crime that went down. If you're not free to leave, you are under arrest whether they say it or not.

Because it is so hard to tell if you are under arrest or not when the cops detain you, you have to do some work to find out. A simple question will do the trick. Whenever you are in police detention and you want to know if you are under arrest, just ask them straight up, "Am I free to leave?" Hopefully when you ask the question they will make it easy for you by saying "yes" or "no." If they say "yes," don't answer any questions and keep it movin'. If they say "no," that means you are under arrest and your rights kick in even if they haven't told you that you are under arrest. We'll explain your rights in detail in the next few sections, but know this for now, whenever you are under arrest, you have the right to remain silent, so shut up!

Back to figuring out if you are under arrest. Always keep in mind that when you ask the police, "Am I free to leave?" they won't usually make it easy for you by saying "yes" or "no." What they will usually do is try to trick you by not answering you directly and then they will go ahead and ask you questions. If they don't answer you directly, just tell them, "Since you haven't told me that I have to stay here and answer your questions, I'm going to go ahead and leave, thanks." Once you tell them, go ahead and leave! If they won't let you leave, you are under arrest and your rights kick in.

Section B: Your Rights During An Arrest

It's time to discuss those rights you have during an arrest. Whenever you are under arrest, you have: 1) the right to remain silent and 2) the right to have your attorney there whenever the cops are asking you questions. These are some important rights because they can be the difference between you doing jail time and you walking free.

Your Right to Remain Silent

Most people are their own worst enemies when dealing with the cops. Never mind snitches, evidence and all of that other stuff, it's your mouth that's most likely to burn you. Yeah that's right, your mouth, not somebody else's. Whenever you talk to the cops, anything you say can and will be used against you later in court. Some folks will tell you that that's not always true. After all, the cops might be trying to solve a case and they might be questioning you as a witness. That may be the case sometimes. Still, some people end up wrongly behind bars because they were trying to be "helpful" to the cops, not knowing that they were suspects or became suspects when they started running their yaps. When the cops arrest you, use your right to remain silent and keep your mouth shut. Then use your right to an attorney by saying, "I would like to speak to an attorney now." Next, tell the police that you won't answer any questions until your attorney is there. Finally, don't say anything until your attorney gets there and you speak to him.

Other than answering basic booking questions at the station or jail, don't answer any questions until you speak to your attorney. Don't talk to the cops while you're in the squad car, at the jail, or any other place, no matter what they say. No matter how badly they try to scare you, no matter if they act really nice to you, no matter if they are the same race, age, or sex as you, no matter if they tell you they can make things easy for you, no matter what—DO NOT TALK TO THE COPS OR ANYBODY ELSE EXCEPT FOR YOUR LAWYER.

If you're thinking, "Wait, I don't have an attorney and can't afford one," don't sweat it. If you can't afford an attorney, the court has to get you one. This guy is called your court-appointed attorney. The one big glitch in needing a court-appointed attorney is that you may not be able to talk to them right away. You might have to sit in a cell for a while, possibly days. Still, do not talk to the cops, prosecutors, judges, bailiffs, guards or any other government person until you've talked to your attorney. In fact, don't even talk to your cellmates because they could be snitchin' to the cops. Just shut the heck up altogether!

Here are some other quick rules that you need to know about arrests:
- The cops always need probable cause to arrest you. That means, they always have to reasonably believe that you committed a crime or are about to commit a crime to arrest you.
- The cops always have to tell you why they are arresting you.
- The cops can arrest you in a public place without an arrest warrant.
- The cops are not allowed to arrest you in your home without an arrest warrant.
- The cops are not allowed to arrest you if you're in somebody else's house without a search and/or arrest warrant (depending on the situation).

Sometimes cops make arrests without an arrest warrant even though they are supposed to get one. When they do, that makes the arrest illegal. Surprisingly, just because the cops arrest you illegally it doesn't mean that they have to let you go. It only

means that any evidence they find during that arrest can't be used against you if you end up going to trial.

TO RECAP

- An arrest is a seizure of you.
- The police can detain you without it being an arrest.
- Police detention becomes an arrest when you are not free to leave whenever you like; even if the police don't tell you that you are under arrest.
- The best way to know if you are free to leave police detention is to ask the police straight up.
- When you are under arrest, you have the right: 1) to remain silent and 2) to have that attorney present while you answer police questions.
- The cops must have probable cause to arrest you just like they do when they seize your stuff.
- The cops always need a warrant to arrest you at home.

Section C: What To Do When The Cops Want To Arrest You At Your House

We told you above that the cops can arrest you in a public place without a warrant but that they need an arrest warrant to arrest you at your house. But, here's what's crazy. They don't need a warrant if you're on your porch or in the doorway of your house. That's right, if you're on your porch or in your doorway, you're not considered in your house. The cops don't need an arrest warrant to snatch you up from any one of those places. All they need is probable cause. Message: make sure you're actually inside your crib if the cops come knockin' without an arrest warrant.

Sometimes, the cops will show up at your house without an arrest warrant and might try to lure you out to arrest you by claiming that they aren't going to arrest you. You have to decide whether to go outside or not. Just remember, if you step outside your house, the cops can and will nab you without an arrest warrant.

What if the cops show up with an arrest warrant? This might seem like strange advice, but if the cops show up at your crib with an arrest warrant you should go with them right then and there and shut the door behind you. Do not, we repeat, do not go back into the house to get anything. See, once the cops got you, they can't let you out of their sight so they're allowed to follow you into the house. If you let the cops into your house, they might find or plant something there that can hurt you in court. You don't want that. The smart thing is to go with the cops right then and there. Yep, just tell them, "Officers, I'm ready to go." Then say, "Officers, I'm remaining silent and I would like to speak to a lawyer now."

Understand, once they've got you, the police are not allowed to go into your house unless they have a search warrant in addition to the arrest warrant. It doesn't matter if you're booty butt naked. Just shut the door behind you and go with them. Don't listen to the cops if they ask you if you want to go in and get some clothes or anything else. Just say "no!" You might be embarrassed because you don't have any clothes on but you'll get over it. Besides, would you rather be embarrassed for a short time or sent to prison for a long time because the cops found or planted something in your house? Plus, the

124

county will provide you with some clothes anyway. They'll probably be nice and colorful, too.

If the cops have an arrest warrant and have to go into your house to get you because you didn't take our advice to immediately go with them, they can pat you down and search anywhere your arms can reach while they're arresting you. They can also search any area you pass by while they're taking you out of the house. They're allowed to do this for protection so that you can't reach out and grab something to bash them with. They're not supposed to be looking for stuff other than weapons that you could reach or evidence you can grab and destroy unless they have a search warrant to look for other things. If they arrest you in your bedroom, they can search your bedroom closet. They can even search a room connected to yours. If they arrest you in the hallway next to your bathroom, they can search the bathroom. If they think that somebody who might mess them up is hiding somewhere in the house, they can search wherever they think the person might be hiding. In other words, they can pretty much search the whole house.

TO RECAP
- **The cops need a warrant to arrest you at your house if you are inside your house. If you are outside your house on the porch or something, all they need is probable cause to snatch you up.**
- **If the cops show up at your house and they have a legit arrest warrant, stay out of the house if possible to keep them from searching your house while arresting you.**

Section D: What To Do When The Cops Want To Arrest You Out Of Your Car

The rules mentioned above apply to arrests made at your car too. When the police stop you on the road, they can search your entire car, mainly because the whole inside of your car is within your reach. What's weird is that unlike your house, the cops can search your car even after making you get out of the car and handcuffing you; even though it would be impossible for you to grab something in the car to hurt them with. Yeah, we know it's stupid that cops can do this. But, a whole lot of criminal law rules are silly. Your car is the danger zone, remember?

Section E: What About Your Friends Getting Arrested At Your House?

OFFICERS PETTI AND GRIMES HAVE A WARRANT TO ARREST CARLOS, BUT ONLY AT HIS HOUSE. UNFORTUNATELY FOR THEM, HE'S NOT AT HIS HOUSE. HE'S AT MALCOLM'S PLAYING MADDEN.

GRIMES AND PETTI KNOW CARLOS IS ALWAYS HANGING OUT AT MALCOLM'S AND THEY FIGURE IF HE'S NOT AT HOME, HE'S PROBABLY THERE.

SO THEY PARK ACROSS THE STREET FROM MALCOLM'S HOUSE TRYING TO DECIDE WHETHER TO GO ASK JUDGE MASTERS FOR A SEARCH WARRANT TO GO AND SEARCH FOR CARLOS AT MALCOLM'S HOUSE. . .

OR TO SAY "SCREW IT" AND ARREST HIM AT MALCOLM'S HOUSE BASED ONLY ON THE ARREST WARRANT THEY HAVE. AFTER THINKING ABOUT IT FOR A FEW MINUTES, BOTH COPS AGREE TO GET CARLOS WITHOUT GOING TO SEE THE JUDGE FOR A SEARCH WARRANT FOR MALCOLM'S HOUSE.

I DON'T FEEL LIKE GOIN' TO THE JUDGE TO GET A DARN SEARCH WARRANT FOR MALCOLM'S HOUSE. LET'S JUST GO ON IN AND NAB CARLOS.

FINE WITH ME. LET'S DO IT!

THEY KNOCK ON MALCOLM'S DOOR.

OPEN UP, POLICE!

Officer Grimes and Officer Petti did an illegal search at Malcolm's house when they went in to get Rob because the arrest warrant for Rob didn't say they could search Malcolm's house to find him. It only said they could go to Rob's house and arrest him. The cops violated Malcolm's rights in this example. That means that the weed that they found can't be used against Malcolm in court. Unless somebody was in danger in Malcolm's house or the officers thought that Rob was destroying evidence, they should have gotten a warrant to search for Rob in Malcolm's house. However, Rob is still done for because the law doesn't have a problem with Rob being arrested from Malcolm's place even though the arrest warrant was only for Rob's place. According to the law, Rob's rights weren't violated, only Malcolm's were.

Even when the cops do have a warrant to properly arrest you at a place, most times they have to announce themselves by yelling something like "Open up, police!" But, like many legal rules there's an exception that helps the cops. The law says that cops don't have to announce themselves if it might endanger their lives. For example, if they think that you might be hiding inside with a 9-mm ready to peel their domes back when they bust in, they can sneak in or bust in without announcing themselves.

TO RECAP
- If the cops arrest somebody else at your house and your house is not listed on their arrest warrant, you can keep any evidence of a crime they find while making the arrest from being used against you in court.
- Cops are supposed to knock and let you know who they are whenever they make an arrest at your house before busting in to get you. But, even if they don't announce themselves before busting in, they can still use any evidence they find.

Section F: Most Are Good Guys, But Some Cops Are Killers

Cops are only supposed to use deadly force if they have good reason to believe that you might seriously hurt or kill them or other people and they reasonably think that they have to use deadly force to arrest you or to keep you from running away. Oh, and most times, if possible, the cops are supposed to warn you before they shoot to kill.

We all know that cops will sometimes use deadly force to make an arrest when they shouldn't. Some use deadly force whenever they feel that they can get away with it. You have to make sure to do your part to stay alive when dealing with those kinds of cops. Please keep in mind that killer cops don't wear signs saying, "I'm a bad cop, BEWARE!" To be on the safe side, you should approach any cop you meet as if he could be a bad cop—meaning don't do anything that might provoke him to unload a clip in you.

Any and all movements, sudden or not, can give a cop reason to kill you. If you find yourself getting arrested you should stay still and relaxed. Only make movements the cop tells you to make. Do not give a cop with an itchy trigger finger and a hard on to dead somebody a so-called "justified" reason to kill you. Don't count on an investigation of a police shooting to keep cops from shooting you. Know this, police investigations will almost always say that a cop was justified in using deadly force. After all, police departments usually investigate themselves. Do you really think they're gonna check themselves?

TO RECAP
- Cops can kill you if they think you may hurt them or someone else and they reasonably think they have to use deadly force to arrest you.
- Cops are supposed to warn you if possible before they use deadly force.

Section G: Racial Profiling Is Okay. If We Lyin', We Flyin'!

Warning, warning!! The government actually allows racist cops to stop and hassle you. Probable cause is all they need for an excuse. You could have a cop, who in his 20 years on the force, has arrested 5,000 black guys and only 5 white guys. The government says that's cool, as long as the black guys gave him probable cause to go after them. Cops don't have to play fair when it comes to choosing who to screw with. We are not makin' this up! Better recognize, it's real in the field.

Because racial and ethnic profiling is especially common while you're driving, you need to avoid giving a racist cop probable cause to mess with you when you're rolling. The best advice we can give you is to obey the traffic laws. That doesn't guarantee that a racist cop won't hassle you, but who knows? It might shrink the chances of it happening. Here are some quick tips to help you avoid becoming a victim of racial profiling when driving:

- Make sure that all of your exterior lights are working right,
- Make sure that you don't have stuff blocking your back window, make sure that none of your windows are tinted too darkly,
- Make certain that your license plate can be seen, and
- Keep your car neat and clean on the inside and out.

Keep everything that's supposed to be inside the car, inside the car (feet, arms, smoke, music, trash). Know that driving around with your music blaring or any type of smoke puffing out of your car is an invitation for the cops to come harass you.

TO RECAP
- A cop can pull you over for racist reasons as long as he has some legit reasons to do so as well, so get with the program and protect yourself.

CHAPTER 13:

THE POLICE OWN THE STREETS

Section A: Reasonable Suspicion Is The Police's Weapon

Your home might be your castle, but the streets belong to the police. Out in the streets, the cops don't need probable cause or a warrant to mess with you.

The police can stop you briefly for a brief pat down and questioning out in public anytime they have a "reasonable suspicion" that you might be involved in, or about to commit a crime. This just means that the cops only need to have a very tiny reason to stop, question, or frisk you. For example, if a cop sees you hanging outside of a store for a long time he might reasonably suspect that you're casing the place. The law allows a cop to count on his experience as a police officer when determining if he has reasonable suspicion. Even though the average person may see you standing outside a store for a long time and think you were just chillin' on the block, a cop can say that in his 20 years of experience on the job, people who hang around stores for a long time usually end up breaking in. Reasonable suspicion is less than probable cause. When the cops see something that they think looks shady, their reasonable suspicion kicks in.

TO RECAP
- If you are in the streets, the cops can stop you, pat you down, and question you briefly if you got shadiness about you.

Section B: The Police Can Grab Your Privates To See What You're Holdin'

The police can also stop and frisk you if they have good reason to believe that you're holding a weapon on you somewhere. And, if while frisking you for a weapon, a cop feels something that seems to be some illegal things, like a bag of weed, pills, stolen property from a crime they know about, etc., they can go all through your pockets. Technically, a cop's only supposed to take weapons or illegal stuff that he can easily feel and tell are weapons or illegal stuff. But, that's hardly ever stopped a cop from seizing other stuff off a suspect. You know the cop is gonna say he felt a weapon or drugs in your pocket even if he really didn't. Until somebody develops a mind reading machine, a cop's word is good enough for most judges.

TO RECAP

- Cops can always pat you down if they have a reasonable suspicion that you are holding that tool on you whenever you are in the streets.

Section C: Them Dang Snitches

The police don't always have to see you do something that looks shady themselves to have reasonable suspicion. They can also have reasonable suspicion if they get a tip from a snitch that something foul is up. If a snitch gives the police a tip that you're up to no good, they can stop you on the street and frisk you. The only thing that keeps any old knucklehead from around the way from lying and setting you up is that the tip has to be from a reliable snitch, and the tip itself has to be reliable. The following are things the law considers when deciding if a tip is reliable or not:

- Did the tip come from a snitch who has given the police good tips before?
- Did the tip predict future events that actually ended up happening?
- Did the snitch give the tip without giving his name, or did he put himself on blast by giving his name and contact information so he could be called on if his information turned out to be wrong?

Section D: You Look Like A Drug Dealer, So You Must Be A Drug Dealer

STOP DRESSING LIKE A THUG! STOP TALKING LIKE A THUG! STOP ACTIN' LIKE A THUG! The reason why we are screaming this at you is that this is how innocent inner city urban people get harassed by the cops over and over again. If you behave like a "typical criminal," the cops can stop and frisk you in a heartbeat. Stop doing everything you hear in them dang rap songs about thuggin'. Take the following example:

Malcolm is listening to his favorite rapper, Cuttanig. Cuttanig says on his latest single, "Jackin' Fools" that he wears his Air Force Ones, his white tee and doo rag whenever he "jacks a fool." Over the last few weeks Officer Petti has been doing some intense investigative police work by listening to several new rap CDs and noting any "criminal language." Cuttanig's CD happens to be in the rotation. Officer Petti makes a note of what Cuttanig says he wears when he's "jackin' fools."

Officer Petti gets a call on the radio about a robbery near the corner of Fifth Street and Crompton Blvd. Apparently some guy got ran for his platinum diamond studded bracelet. Suddenly, Officer Petti recalls seeing some young guys on the corner of Fifth and Crompton who wear "thug" gear; the same kind that Cuttanig described in his No. 1 hit. Naturally, Officer Petti makes a beeline straight to the corner looking for anybody wearing white tees, Air Force Ones, and doo rags.

Malcolm, who's known around town for wearing whatever's the "hotness" decides to hit the corner store for a soda and chips. He throws on his crisp extra baggy pair of jeans making sure that they have just the right amount of sag, his XXXXXXXXXXXXXXXXXXL Hanes white tee, and his Carolina blue Air Force Ones. He also makes sure to ice his wrist up with the new platinum diamond studded bracelet that he bought by working extra shifts for five months at Mickey D's, just in case he runs into some fine females on the way. The honeys love the ice! Malcolm heads out the door.

As luck would have it, as Malcolm is nearing the corner of Fifth and Crompton, Officer Petti's squad car pulls up next to the curb. Rushing out of the car, Officer Petti runs up on Malcolm and starts questioning him about the robbery.

Malcolm thinks this is some bullcrap, but Officer Petti is going to say that he has reasonable suspicion to check Malcolm because of Malcolm's "thug" gear, his location, and the piece of jewelry that fits the description of the stolen jewelry. And, Officer Petti is going to be right.

Unfortunately for Malcolm, the law will agree with Officer Petti. We can already hear the complaints, "I should be able to wear what I want. How the cops gonna mess with me just 'cause of my clothes?" What do you want us to say? Yeah, that's unfair, but that's life.

Just know that the law allows the cops to mess with you based on how you dress and act even if they don't directly see you doin' dirt. Dress like a D-Boy and the cops will hassle you like one. In fact, cops pretty much get a free pass to mess with people who fit a drug-courier profile. A drug-courier profile is a usual set of behaviors of people who traffic drugs. If you fit a drug-courier profile, the police are basically allowed to go all out on you with a stop and search. A drug-courier profile usually includes the following:

- The types of clothes that a drug dealer usually wears (white tees, Air Force Ones, hoodies, and other stuff you see the D-Boys wearing)

- The way drug dealers wear their clothes (baggy jeans sagging off the butt, long white tees that look like dresses, baseball caps pointed to the side of town they reppin', grillz)

- The types of places drug dealers usually go (drug houses, the D-Boy's house, strip clubs, the drug corner, major drug source cities like Miami)

- The types of vehicles drug dealers use to get around (black SUVs, especially with 22s or larger, vehicles with tinted windows)

- The people drug dealers hang with (other drug dealers, drug fiends, high school dropouts, convicted felons)

- Odd behaviors (driving an $80,000 car when they don't have a regular job, making a lot of short phone calls to the same phone numbers, paying for plane tickets in all cash, going to and from abandoned houses or abandoned apartments all the time).

We'll say it again, stop doing what the D-Boys do! It will get you caught up by the police. Oh, and a quick side note so you know. Wearing your pants sagging off your butt is not hot! It's what ex-cons do as a habit because they couldn't wear belts while they were locked up. Stop doing stuff you don't really understand. If you ain't in prison, stop actin' like you are. Wear a belt. It will make it easier to run if you need to!

TO RECAP
- **The way you look and act can give the police reasonable suspicion to get up in your grill.**

- The people you hang with and the places you go can give the police reasonable suspicion to get up in your grill.
- If you "gangsta" you "gangsta," and the cops can get all up in that grill. So, don't be complainin' when it happens.

Section E: You're A 'Hood Because You Hang In The 'Hood

Ok, now here comes some real foul stuff so brace yourself. The law says that if you are in a so-called "high-crime" area, and you run when you see the cops coming, the cops can stop you and frisk you. The cops usually claim you wouldn't run if you didn't do anything. Even though we all know that's crap, according to the law, being in a high crime area and running when you see the boys gives them the right to stop you.

This really blows because most people who live in "high crime" areas don't live there by choice. Can you go hang out somewhere away from your "high crime" hood; somewhere safer like say, the suburbs? Nope, because surprisingly, the cops are allowed to stop you if you "appear" to be somebody that isn't usually found in a certain area; you know, like being Black or Latino in a predominantly white suburb. You can't hang out around your own neighborhood, and you can't go chill in the suburbs because you are a criminal suspect just for being a minority out there. Discrimination is alive and well, folks, please believe.

TO RECAP
- Just hangin' in the hood gives the cops reasonable suspicion to stop and harass you.
- Hangin' in the 'burbs when you don't look like you are from there gives the cops reasonable suspicion to harass you.

134

CHAPTER 14:

TAKING ON THE GOVERNMENT

Now that you know there are rules the cops have to follow whenever they try to search or arrest you, what you need to know next is what to do when they don't follow those rules. The Constitution doesn't allow the cops to use anything against you that it got by violating the rules on searches and arrests. When the rules aren't followed, you can fight to have any evidence collected against you kept out of court so it can't be used against you at your trial. The less evidence against you that a judge or jury is allowed to see, the better your chances of walking.

If the police searched your house without a warrant when they were supposed to get one and they find some evidence of a crime to use against you, you can ask the judge to throw that evidence out of court. If it's thrown out, the prosecutor won't be able to present it to the jury while trying to prove that you committed a crime. See the following example to get an idea of what we are talking about:

Officer Petti and Officer Grimes are investigating a jewelry store robbery. They get a hot tip from a snitch that Malcolm committed the robbery and that the jewels are in the top drawer of a dresser in Malcolm's bedroom. Instead of going to Judge Masters to show him their reasons and to ask for a warrant to search Malcolm's bedroom, Officer Petti and Officer Grimes drive straight over to Malcolm's, walk up to his door, and bust in on Malcolm while he's playing Grand Theft Auto with his friends. Malcolm asks the officers to leave but they just push him aside, walk to his bedroom and begin searching through his drawers for the jewels. They end up finding the jewels and Malcolm is shocked because he had no idea the jewels were in there. He had been set up by his homie Rob who just so happens to be the snitch. The officers go ahead and arrest Malcolm for robbery and take him to jail for trial.

At Malcolm's trial, his defense attorney asks Judge Masters to throw out the evidence that the jewels were found in the drawer in Malcolm's bedroom. Malcolm's defense attorney explains to Judge Masters that Officer Petti and Officer Grimes found the jewels in violation of the search rules by not getting a search warrant. Judge Masters agrees that the officers should have come to him to get a search warrant and because they broke the rules, the jewels they found in the drawer in Malcolm's house had to be thrown out and kept from the jury. After getting the evidence of the jewels thrown out, Malcolm's defense attorney then asks Judge Masters to dismiss the charges against

Malcolm because the police technically don't have any evidence against him to show to the jury since the jewels aren't in the trial anymore. Agreeing with Malcolm's defense attorney again, Judge Masters dismisses the charges against Malcolm and sets him free.

If you are able to show that the police didn't follow the rules, it could mean that you go free! You best keep track of everything that happens when you encounter the police and be on the look out for their slip-ups. Honestly, there are so many rules that they are supposed to follow, that the chances are good that they are going to screw up somewhere and give you an out. It just comes down to you being smart enough to catch the screw-up and telling your lawyer about it in detail. Here are some tips for keeping track of whether the cops are following the rules. Some of these you've already heard but we'll list them again here.

- Find out if they have a legit warrant to search or arrest you.
- Read the warrant closely and see if the places they end up searching are listed on the warrant.
- Read the warrant closely and see if the things they are searching for are listed on the warrant and could actually be found in those places. For example, they shouldn't be searching for a rifle in the glove box of your car because there's no way it could fit inside there.
- Read the warrant closely and see if the things they take are actually listed on the warrant.
- Pay attention to how rough the cops get with you when trying to search or arrest you.
- Take note of the time of day it is when the search happens. Is it in the middle of the night or during the day?
- Pay attention to whether they just busted into your spot to do the search without any warning, or if they knocked, yelled out "Police" and asked to come in and do the search.
- Whenever you are being searched or stopped without a warrant, keep track of how long they keep you from leaving.
- Whenever a search or arrest is over, as soon as you find yourself with some free time, write down exactly what happened, how it happened, when it happened, who was there, and what was said. This will keep you from forgetting important facts that could be helpful later when you try to get evidence thrown out of court.

TO RECAP
- If the police don't follow the rules that they are supposed to follow when they do a search, or when they arrest you and take your stuff, you can have any evidence they find against you thrown out of court.
- Be smart and take notes about what's going down as you are being searched and/or arrested so you don't forget things that could help you get off.
- Tell your attorney about everything that happened when the cops were handling you, even if you aren't sure if they broke the rules.

CONCLUSION:

THE POWER IS YOURS; USE IT RIGHT

The world of criminal law and criminal procedure is very tricky. And, it can be a very dangerous world to be in if you don't know what you're doing. In When The Cops Come Knockin', we explained what it takes to commit crimes, how to defend yourself against criminal charges, what your rights against government violation are, and how to assert and protect those rights. You have gained power now that you have read When The Cops Come Knockin' and you have a better understanding of what criminal law and criminal procedure are all about.

However, your newly found power is only going to be useful to you and those you care about if you use it wisely. Although you may have learned a few tricks to keep law enforcement from doing things like searching your stuff when they don't have a right to or arresting you when they aren't supposed to, the best thing you can do to stay out of trouble is to follow the laws. Once the wheels of justice start turning against you, the outcome is always going to be up in the air no matter how much you know about the law. And, if you are poor or a minority, things are going to be slanted against you.

Even though you've probably heard it a thousand times before, we're going to tell you once again to chill out on the drug-dealing. You are going to get caught no matter how clever and gangsta you think you are. There is no way around it. It's like how you can go a whole year without catching a cold or the flu. You may not get sick for a whole year, hell, maybe even a couple of years. But, as long as you keep living, you will eventually get sick because you can't avoid all the chances to catch a cold forever. There are people in the world that do nothing but figure out how to get you on a drug charge. They may screw-up and miss you one hundred times, but if you keep going, they are eventually going to outsmart you, or get lucky at the very least. And, when they do, they are going to nail you to the wall. All it takes is one time.

Cool out on the violence. Or at least stop being a idiot. Quit carrying your heater and knuckle up! Whenever you get into a fight, or even whenever you raise your voice and threaten to whup somebody's butt, you could be sent to jail. Whenever you carry a gun you are setting yourself up to do 20 to life. Add a gun to a simple fist fight and you end up with a murder charge. Because, if a dude is kickin' your butt, you know you ain't gonna let him get away with it if you have a gun on you. You're probably gonna smoke 'em. But, here's a news flash. Shooting somebody who gave you a beat-down won't change the fact that you got beat down. And, if you pull a gun out without even trying to fight first, you are just a punk.

Quit taking the "easy way." The easy money from drug dealing and robbing, the easy clothes from shoplifting, the easy way of getting that DVD player for cheap by buying it from the hookup man—stop all that stuff. The come-ups are where the cops like to set traps to catch you. Stop thuggin'! A slick enough police officer and prosecutor can throw you in prison for years just for thuggin' if they really want to.

Ladies, stop showin' so much love to thugs so dang much! Show some love to the regular 9-to-5 brother. He's moving slow, but he's gonna be that dude with a good job and benefits that won't give you the time of day while your thuggin' man will be in jail running up your phone bill on collect calls talkin' bout, "Don't you be sexin' nobody else while I'm in here." You may think he's tough cause he be runnin' around the 'hood punkin' everybody, but please believe he'll be getting punked when he lands in max security prison.

Keep thinkin' your thug is different if you want to. He's going to jail. If you don't believe it, go talk to five females that are 5 or 10 years older than you and ask them where their thuggin' boyfriends from five or ten years ago are right now. Then ask them where the straight-laced dudes that used to have crushes on them are right now.

If you've kept your nose clean and still find yourself on the wrong end of the law facing down some serious criminal stuff, remember the power you've gotten from When The Cops Come Knockin' and be strong. Be on the lookout for When The Cops Come Knockin' Volume II: Snatched Up for info on the game once you've been arrested. Until then, if you are ever arrested, keep your mouth shut and ask for an attorney. You have both the right to keep quiet and the right to speak to an attorney, but that's just the tip of the iceberg when it comes to being arrested. We'll put you up on the game in Volume II.

ABOUT THE AUTHORS

Travis T. Townsend, Jr.— is a practicing attorney with experience in criminal, corporate transactional, and securities law. Mr. Townsend received his Bachelor of Arts degree in the social science of Psychology from the University of Michigan School of Literature, Science and Arts in 2000. Mr. Townsend received his law degree from the prestigious University of Michigan School of Law in 2003. Travis was raised in the small urban town of Muskegon Heights, Michigan, where many of the families live below the national poverty level and parents often work multiple jobs to make ends meet. During his tenure at the University of Michigan Law School, Travis quickly learned that many common behaviors that were acceptable in his neighborhood were actually teetering on the criminal. Travis recognized that many of the youths and young adults living in such environments are often unaware of the criminal nature of their activities, and as a result, find themselves in the clutches of the criminal justice system. Travis connected the dots and came to the conclusion that a number of good people generate criminal records and spend time in prison due to a lack of resources and an inability to hire adequate legal counsel. In an attempt to increase understanding of criminal law amongst poorer individuals, Travis decided it was time someone wrote a book that would break down criminal law in a simple way for all to interpret, and to provide it in a cost effective manner. So, Travis joined forces with his brother, Trinity, who shared many experiences with Travis growing up, as well as the realizations reached during Trinity's own matriculation through the Emory School of Law to create *When The Cops Come Knockin'*.

Trinity Townsend — is an attorney and former high school teacher who resides in Atlanta, Georgia. He is a graduate of the University of Michigan School of Education and the Emory University School of Law. Trinity shares many of the reasons as his brother, Travis, for writing this book. As a teacher Trinity saw firsthand how unsuspecting youth often find themselves on the wrong side of the law, mostly because of ignorance. Writing *When The Cops Come Knockin'* provided Trinity with an opportunity to help young (and older) people avoid trouble with the legal system by explaining the system and how it works. By drawing on his teaching experience as well as his experience working with a state public defenders agency, his goal in writing When The Cops Come Knockin' is to provide a powerful tool that will prevent people from getting caught up in the criminal justice system in the first place.

(Copy this form)
Quick Order Form

For credit card orders, please visit our website at:
www.copscomeknockin.com

To order by mail, you may use this form. Please make your check or money order payable to: *Torinity, LLC.*

Name: _____

Address: _____

City: _____ State: ____ Zip: _____

Telephone: _____

Email address: _____

Item	Price	Quantity	Totals
Cops Come Knockin'	**$19.95**		
Sales Tax 7% (Georgia Residents)			
Shipping and handling in the U.S.: $4.00 for first book and $2.00 for each additional book.			
S&H International: $9.00 for first book; $5.00 for each additional.			
		Total	

Please send your order to : Torinity Publishing Company
3645 Marketplace Blvd.
Suite 130-333
East Point, GA 30344

Or Call 1-800-552-0762

I understand that I may return the book(s) within 30 days
for a full refund.

CPSIA information can be obtained at www.ICGtesting.com
226342LV00001B/13/P